In Search of Sanctuary

Wildlife, My Teacher

Brendan Price

Strategic Book Publishing and Rights Co.

Strategic Book Publishing and Rights Co., LLC
USA | Singapore
www.sbpra.com

For information about special discounts for bulk purchases, please contact Strategic Book Publishing and Rights Co., LLC Special Sales, at bookorder@sbpra.net.

ISBN: 978-1-68181-219-9

To Mary, Cormac, Orla, my family, Muse, mentors and friends, and to my fellow creatures, great and small … thanks for all the stories.

Author's Note
A glossary is provided at the end of the book for all text denoted with an asterisk.

CONTENTS

PREFACE

Life and history, for many, are charted by milestone events and benchmarks separated by tedious, ticking time. These benchmarks most often occur between the infinite small events that are a part of day-to-day living. This collection of stories relates some such "inch marks" that have charted the path of my life, leading me here. Animals feature in them all.

Great events give a sense of occasion for many, marking time and position—the when and where of our lives—but do not tell the how and why we came to that place at that point in time.

Mortar between bricks gives a wall its substance. Space between stones gives life to a river bed. The innumerable, unmeasurable little events between milestones, like stars in constellation, bring us to life's landmarks, or "inch marks" to milestones. A great work of art starts with simple brushstrokes and, with that, maybe the seed of a thought in an artist's mind, impulse inspired before that by, perhaps, the tiniest of events.

This collection of stories is a small sample about such events, involving obscure animals, which came to define my life as an animal handler.

I believe for everyone it is the same: if we pause to reflect, it is the many tiny events that shape and define the person we become, and the exchange of such stories is what makes it so exciting as we get to know one another.

For the chef, the poet, the farmer, the fisherman, the day labourer, the friend, partner, spouse, parent and child, it is the same. "Inch marks" put milestones in perspective and offer a qualitative measure of life, making more sense of quantitative leaps.

Life is made up of such stories, and history is abundant with such memories of detail, blazing a trail to historical treasure trove and leaving tracks for others to follow. My trail led from the primordial ooze of the mud and clay, weeds, vegetable patch and bushes of my back garden, to the rivers, hills and coast around Dublin.* These experiences brought me to the world of zoos and captivity, wildlife rescue and rehabilitation, and ultimately, to the world of policy and diplomacy surrounding wildlife protection, sustainability, and human rights.

Wildlife are ambassadors for our natural world. They are the "canary in the mine" and the most efficient and economic indicators of the health of our "life-support" systems. What ails them ails humanity and, what's more, they hold the secrets to living sustainably and harmoniously on Earth, our home.

In every story I have been led by animals. They are companions on a journey who make the miles go faster and the journey less arduous.

I hope you enjoy these stories of some of my "inch marks" as much I as enjoyed the experiences detailed herein.

Brendan Price

Prologue: Why I Write

This must be the most difficult thing I've ever tried to express.

The stories to follow are simple and representative of a life's learning curve, through associations with animals.

Many of us require special avenues for learning, wisdom, and enlightenment. I can imagine no other experiences to have led me thus, and I vehemently uphold the role of animals and nature in our society, whose education can only be enriched by such tutors.

But back to the blank sheet, and why …

I'm not moved to become a literary figure or I'd have written long before now. I don't fit Orwell's* Four Motives theory. I have little wisdom to impart that is not better spoken than written, better lived than spoken, and learned by first-hand experience and from the animals themselves.

If I do their wisdom justice, as simple scribe, maybe it encourages others to follow and journey for themselves.

I've no desire to leave a lasting legacy. Many civilisations came and went without leaving written record. My work was my art and craft, ephemeral though that is. Much like a fleeting "butterfly summer", if it brought smiles and left memories, and some poor creature had an extra day of life and fulfilment, wasn't that enough?

The beauty and fulfilment was in the doing—working hand-to-hand, head-to-head and heart-to-heart with another creature trying to live another day. And even if things are pre-determined and our time of death determined by fate, aren't we all best fulfilled by resisting it to the last?

My introductions to most people were over animals, their rescues and releases, and the message between the covers of this book may introduce me to more such unique and wonderful people, even after I am long gone. I hope such readers enjoy it.

So, who's special? Well, I'm the result of somebody else whose story is part writ on me. Next, my wife Jack and I took up with each other, sharing probably the first responsibility of our lives. Then there was Bubble and Squeak, a strong son and a golden princess, the results of our lives. They now sing off a different sheet and write off a different page, the one a better zoologist than I could ever be, and the other a greater human rights and justice advocate than I could ever hope to be.

And so, because of these afore referenced shared and inherited experiences, I write for all, not to be understood but to assist understanding of all the great cosmic questions still awaiting answers. As I trundle along my own little rat track, my eyes are lifted to the heavens. I'm reminded of fellow creatures sharing understanding with me and I can write, where many may not express in such format.

It is out of love and a duty to share what was shared with me, ever aware in the utterance of Joe Smart,* an "animal man" and teacher, that as clay we're "not yet ready for the maker's hand."

I hope you enjoy these reflections and the people and animals who inspired them.

Grand Central *Budlia*

As a child this appeared the busiest airport in the world and, to this day, infinitely more exotic than any other I have seen.

It was the ambition of every first generation Dublin urbanite to have a garden, and in Dublin's first suburbs, everyone was first generation, from either the inner city or rural Ireland and then homogenised like the new milk of today.

Many of us knew not more than a couple of generations whence we came, as many identities, roots and records were lost in the Custom House burning in May of 1921, at the peak of the Irish Civil War.

Our gardens set us apart and were conversation pieces across walls and hedges. Privet hedges, sweet smelling in summer and full of sparrows, box hedges, grisselinia, escallonia, and fuchsia—all were in the mix—mostly aliens, but we were trying to rise from hungry grass and poverty. Vegetable gardens and allotments, to supplement meagre wages, were punishing, if rewarding.

And gardening fervour reached to lawns, a few flowers, and shrubs, as people rose above subsistence. Lawns had to be like bowling greens and this brought out the daisy-killer in the adults, while children loved to make daisy chains, May altars and perfumes from these and other wildflowers not tolerated by adults and unobserved even from the cultivated petals guarded by them. Perfumes were

3

jam jars full of assorted petals in water! Gates were closed at night against wandering tinkers' horses.

In the days before celebrity gardeners and themed gardens, a resident would be known as much by a dog or specific prize plant as surname or postal address. One had a cherry, another crab apple, another almond blossom or magnolia, and so it went. Some even had roses.

My father had planted a small innocuous shrub with silver-grey hastate foliage in a prized corner at the front of the house, catching the sun from noon onwards and it grew with us as children, far more vigorously than he anticipated or planned. In mid-summer, it would produce spikelet's which grew to massive, cone-shaped clusters of tiny mauve goblet shaped flowers, each little receptacle producing a minute quantity of intoxicating nectar. Even the fuchsia producing drinkable quantities of nectar for children could not rival the drawing power of this hairy grey bush.

As the bush blossomed, we watched and waited for the great natural phenomenon to follow, the aerial invasion of our front garden by every flying creature known in this part of the world. There were admirals, peacocks, cabbage whites, bees, wasps, hover-flies, and moths and bats at night. It was one of the great movements of nature, akin to wildebeest or monarch butterfly migrations, and it was in our front garden.

And with their arrival, came all the children of the road, with their jam jars and nets, to our garden.

Beautiful butterflies were captured and kept on display in jam jars till wilting in the heat or released by a child of advanced sensibility. Honey bees were gathered and "fed" flowers. Solitary bumble bees and angry wasps were another target, setting the jars buzzing and vibrating.

As the tree grew heavier with flower, more and more came by innumerable aerial pathways, never crashing, never colliding. The bush "buzzed" with crypto-jargon, and little messengers lured to the elixir carried off secret code genetic messages to pollinate other flowers.

Advanced children mixed species in their jam jar laboratories—a bumble bee and a butterfly, a wasp and a honey bee—in serious scientific enquiry to no known end.

The dogs of the road would follow the children, and a hunter pride surrounded the bush daily. Occasionally a barking dog, frenzied by the "buzz saw" insects, would snap too well and recoil, yelping when stung in the mouth. Children, too, were casualties from time to time and retired, temporarily crying, but returned rapidly, so strong was the lure of the insect oasis and addictive was the hunt. Mothers would cajole *wains** against the hunt, but the lust was too much for primitive hunters and they'd return time and again, till colder, wetter weather and fading flowers ended the chase. And the end for *Budlia*, like the great bison of the US plains, was spiritless and full of desolation.

Mid-summer madness became a thing of memory and story as schools reopened and autumn, then winter, followed.

Budlia was not a bush but a place of great biodiversity, drawing life from an alien root. It was a summer scientific field station and battle ground of many species, and in winter, a stalk-stemmy ghost. As we passed it on our way to school in winter, we knew phoenix-like, it would rise, bud, and flower again.

Unlike rhododendron and garden exotics to follow, it knew its place and role of support for native wildlife. Later we learned botanical names, classification, and ecological roles, but *Budlia* remains a place of sanctuary for wildlife and naturalists during childhood.

ONLY THE RIVER RAN FREE

My father grew up at the Dodder Falls in Beaver Row, just upstream from Donnybrook* Church and the site of the old Fayre, which lent its bastardised name to the conqueror's language. While the *Gall** took our language, the *Gael** enriched theirs!

Dublin was bounded to the south by the Dodder and to the north by the Tolka rivers in those days, with the Liffey central and dividing the city north and south. Beyond those rivers were the country and new suburbs.

Some of my earliest memories were of going to school on the cross-bar of my father's bicycle or seated on the tank of his motor-bike, and the most exciting part of the run was down the hill and across the Dodder Bridge to Milltown.

The river was strictly out of bounds and so, de facto, a great attraction for young break-aways from the regimentation of national school, blackboards and chalk, marla,* old maids, and nuns—kindly folk all but constraints to any growing young boy.

One day we did not return home from school, setting off a search along the river. We were grounded after that!

Tinkers in roll-top caravans or under tarpaulin camped by the river and the tinker women came around the new houses regularly. My mother, as many of her neighbours, had her lady and they'd have tea in the kitchen together and the visitor would go away with

6

a bag, till the next week. My mother and the ladies of the neighbourhood enjoyed those visits.

Occasionally the tinkers' horses—great hairy creatures—many piebald and skewbald, would also visit the gardens to feed on new lawn, if gates were left open.

Bread, milk, and coal would also come to the houses, drawn by horse and cart, and these could be heard from early mornings. A loose horseshoe would always sing out. Bigger animals these, with feathered feet, they never left the stays of their carts.

If you were not awake early, blue tits would crack the foil coverings of the milk bottles for a sup of cream from the top, leaving less for the porridge.

Life was an orderly arrangement around work, shopping, school times, and meals, interrupted by these regular and frequent visitors. Men went to jobs five days and more a week, women saw children to school and walked into the city, carrying bags and pushing infants in prams to shop, to then return home, and prepare food before school let out.

The women raised us till the fathers came home, and then we had to account for our day.

Saturday was for home and garden and Sunday for rest, mass, newspapers, comics, and sweets.

City, suburbs, and country were all compartmentalised and connected. Only the river and river residents moved freely.

* * *

There was a dog at almost every house, a vegetable garden to tend, and flowers and pets as time, tenure, and resources allowed.

As a child, occasionally my father would take me on a great wildlife expedition, allowing my mother to rest a few hours, and we would go to the river where he caught salmon as a child.

Sometimes we went to the small fall, other times to the Beaver Row Falls, when not in flood.

When the river was in flood, you could only watch and listen to the Beaver Row Falls from a safe distance, as the cascading water weaved rainbows from spray and air and sunlight on fine days and smoke and mist from thundering water on grey ones.

Those other times, when the river was calm, we'd find quiet pools beneath the falls, teeming with minnow, scarce later like sparrows in the city. With little nets and jam jars on strings, we'd catch the minnow for a few hours and bring them home.

He taught me patience and respect and would catch more quietly than I could hastily. They were wonderful quarry, sensing every shadow, fast movement, and clumsy grab, eluding me more often than not! In an instant a pool would empty of minnow by any clumsy move and they'd disappear into the fast running water of the river, not to return till danger was passed.

The minnows would come with us to live for the next week in a basin in the garden, in the shelter of some stones and feed on bread crumbs. Each day I could observe them until they returned to their home the following weekend or earlier of a summer's evening, if the water temperature had been climbing.

They were lightning fast and really only visible when stationary. How they propelled from point to point without being seen, was miraculous. Faster than light and invisible in motion, these were the quarks and Higgs boson particles of the day!

As I grew, the river became poisoned and all but dead with a paper factory and laundry, and only in flood over the falls did it still seem truly alive. For years it flowed yellow, frothing over the falls with an ochre fog hanging over it at night from the factory exhausts and lights.

My father took me then on longer expeditions to rock pools and harbour walls by the coast, progressing to crabs and later mackerel and ultimately losing all my acquired fishing tackle by foul-hooking a basking shark swimming into Skerries* Harbour one stormy day.

With time and pollution awareness, the river recovered somewhat and I'd see my red-haired cousins fly-fishing it again for trout, and again, they told me there are pools of minnow, mallard, and heron to be seen, and even alien terrapins, basking on the banks in high summer.

Still the river in momentary wildness breaks its banks in flood, defying years of successive engineering attempts to contain it.

Maybe someday runs of salmon will be seen again leaping the falls.

THE SPARROWLANDS

The new estates and gardens growing outwards from the city cover much farmland, hedgerow, and sportive wood and builders left great scars on the earth.

New residents were industriously backfilling this with top soil and spoil, and salvaging anything remotely transportable by hand, bucket, barrow, bicycle or *bogey*.* Even prams were commissioned and infants temporarily parked elsewhere. Top soil was most in demand and would disappear as quickly as a mound would appear, borne away ant-like by lean and hungry men with barrows.

Builder's debris, off-cuts, and packaging were all borne off by the armies of part-time gardeners for fencing, cloches, lazy beds, and even ramshackle sheds. Even nails were pulled and straightened for further use.

The displaced wildlife moved farther into the foothills of the mountains, apart from the sparrows, which fighting a rear-guard action, picked among the torn, poached, and puddled landscape close to the households. They colonised the eaves of the houses, awaiting the opportunity to reclaim the emerging gardens and hedgerows. They forged a symbiotic relationship with the new inhabitants.

While the land was barren after the builders and the new residents were feverishly engaged in remedial work to bring it back into production to supplement kitchen budgets and tables, the sparrows eked out a living complemented by crumbs.

Bread was a big component of family diets then and before sliced pans, batch loaves, and vacuum-packed bread, crumbs were much more abundant and were religiously put out for the sparrows, who'd swoop down out of nowhere in tight little flocks in flight formation to clean them up as quick as they landed.

Even stale bread wasn't wasted! Mostly it went to bread puddings transformed warm and soggy by milk and raisins, topped off with a sticky Demerara sweet crust to delight children—the ultimate reward for clean plates and eaten dinner! And if there was more, it and the scrapings of the baking dish, also went to the sparrows.

On the occasions a cake flopped or burned in the oven this, too, would be offered to the sparrows, setting off a feeding frenzy and drawing in other fly-over flocks from all around. The cake would shrink as we watched; disappearing faster than any household could have eaten it and the pleasure of watching the joyous feast was some compensation for the loss.

Horse manure in the suburbs, still plentiful enough before the demise of the working horse, was another staple of the sparrows and they'd descend on these offerings, as the milk, bread, and other assorted horse carts, went house to house and peck, pick, scatter, and sift the dung for the hayseed within.

The sparrows were our constant and only wild companions, while the "bad lands" were recovering.

We'd heard stories of sparrows caught for food during the ration-ing years* and young children had a tradition of trying to trap them in the Sparrowlands, between the rows of housing. The traps took the form of a box, held at a tilt by a stick, attached to a string, and trailing back a safe distance to a place of concealment.

The excitement and anticipation of children was palpable and knuckles whitened, holding motionless to the end of the string, awaiting the descent of the flock. Crumbs were the bait, scattered about and leading under the shadow of the box to the ultimate and last free feast.

But it was as if the sparrows knew, seeing the unusually quiet children, who'd normally be chattering like them. They were too fast and all too often the string jerked and the box fell on vacated space! The children would carefully, in hope, feel inside the box before lifting it, in case by freak chance one had been too slow or caught off guard. Eventually they'd give up the exercise, confounded by a smarter quarry. With repeated failed attempts it seemed the sparrows grew smarter and smarter, returning quicker each time to nonchalantly hopping, chattering, and feeding about the box, yet never tempting the overhanging trap.

One day a blue budgerigar flew in with a flock, causing great excitement. It transpired it had fled the cage of an elderly neighbour and she had a bounty out for its recapture.

Frustrated trappers were roused within the body "childhood," and the most sophisticated and delicately balanced box traps ever conceived were brought into play. These were hair-trigger affairs and the trappers were focussed like never before.

For some days the little flock came to feed with the bright blue budgerigar in their midst. The first attempt to spring the trap had failed, but the children noted the budgerigar's preoccupation with food, dulled flight responses, and poorer take-off. The long tapering wings and low undercarriage were an impediment to swift take-off and he could not turn as deftly as the swarthier sparrows. The children plotted to respond accordingly.

For the next few days, the birds were left to feed undisturbed, even in the shadow of the box, and they dared to venture farther each time. The normality and chatter of children in the open, feigning disinterest, relaxed even the sparrows and on-looking mothers, who always had a third eye for children congregating about some grand enterprise.

And so high noon approached in the Sparrowlands and the daily crumbs had been spread as the little flock flew in with the blue stranger amidst them. They hoovered around the crumbs near the box, carelessly following the trail under the shadowed maw of the trap, and were feeding confidently on the bounty within when the trap snapped closed.

Neither bird nor adult had even noticed a child move into position to jerk the string! The sparrows disappeared for the rest of the day, but when the oldest child felt tentatively, sightlessly within the box and clutched onto a little, flapping, protesting, muscular, feathery body, they knew they had been successful. The child pinioned the wings tightly in a little hand, disregarding the eighty pounds per square inch pressure beak, sinking into an index finger and drawing warm blood, and so drawing the bird from the box for all to see—a mighty angry, blue budgerigar!

Ignoring the pain and indignation, neither child nor budgerigar relaxed their grip, till the troop of children marched down the road to return the feathered fury to his doting mistress and cage. His name was Benny and his ancestors came from Australia. Spirited though he was, he'd not have lasted in the Sparrowlands.

Bounty and sweets were rightfully claimed, and a joyous, tearful old lady reunited with her reluctant but beloved companion.

Budgies are southern hemisphere birds, occupying similar niche to our sparrows in our northern hemisphere. They rank as one of the world's most intelligent birds by even human intelligence quotient criteria. But it was the sparrows who defied the trap, continued to fly free, and delight children and adults for years to follow.

In time the Sparrowlands became fertile and prosperous, but the sparrows mysteriously flew the city and suburbs almost overnight. Only small pockets remained. Further waves of succession and colonisation by swathes of other species followed. Natives returning, exotics, aliens, feral and domestic, flora and fauna of unprecedented diversity in new and ground-breaking relationships were creating a new ecosystem between the rows of houses.

The flight of the sparrows was like the loss of the dinosaurs—entire species removed from the fauna of the suburbs and much of the city. Was it the loss of the crumbs and horse shit, the flourishing gardens conferring advantage on other species, new predators, cataclysmic climatic or environmental change leading to extirpation and extinction of species in the suburbs?

The dowdy little brownies still cheer and delight where enclaves remain and they still like crumbs. What they lacked in colour and ornamentation was more than compensated for in resilience and character.

Did they leave us or did we lose them?

JELLIES

The seasons of childhood memory are a parallel universe and often differ greatly from historical or meteorological record.

When schools broke up for holidays, summers hung lazily over Dublin and space and time seemed immeasurably expanded.

Dublin was blessed among capital cities of the globe, nestled around the bay, fed by rivers, with the mountains to its back, and a temperate climate made for near perfection in this natural playground.

With children loosed from the shackles of schooling, free to explore and learn, opportunities and horizons were infinite.

Among the mountains and Pine Forest, every ridge crested and clearing reached gave view to endless more peaks rolling out in the distance. We knew from lessons and stories this mountainous terrain harboured freedom fighters in the time before independence. History and childhood imaginings forged that same sense of independence among children that would be defended again, against all invasion or threat. The wildness of the places nurtured the growing independence of the children.

But in the hot, hazy summer days, it was to the beaches and coast all were drawn, to that line of tide, where the rest of the world met the boundaries of our island home.

On awakening, those early days of the school holidays, refreshed from the exhaustion and endeavours of each day previous, the sun seemed always up ahead of us and high in the sky. Children wolfed down breakfast to get moving and catch up on the day down by the seashore.

Older children walked and cycled to the coast. Younger ones were pushed in prams and buggies by mothers, occasionally abandoning the day's labours to bring food and drink in big shopping bags. They could use buses to get to the coast.

On weekends fathers would join the migration to the coast and the few cars about would share and be crammed with children.

There were also beaches aplenty beyond Dublin Bay and these could be reached by bus and train. The train ride along the East Coast remains the most attractive train journey in Ireland's rail network.

If you were really lucky in the long summers, you got to holiday awhile somewhere around the coast of Ireland in a caravan or rented cottage, with country relatives or youth clubs or the Sunshiners.* The Sunshiners would organise bands of children to get out of the City for a seaside holiday.

In high summer everybody wanted to escape the City for a while, to be beside the sea. Dublin Bay was accessible and always there for us.

On weekends family units and extended families arrived at the coast, like an invasion force, establishing beachheads, laying out rugs and towels, and erecting windbreaks. Once territory and shelter were secured, a chore from which children had fled into the water, field kitchens were established and rations distributed to returning hungry children.

Weekdays were different, as the coast was more the domain of older children, roaming in groups and gangs free to range and explore beyond parental controls. These were akin to tribes, loosely led, operating mainly by consensus, and organised by a primitive colony brain. Fed early in the mornings before being discharged from homes for the day, they raced across beaches, scrabbled over rocks, dived and plunged in pools, and swam in the shallows, competing and stretching each other in every *dering-do* act and moment.

Once they had their space, they cautiously avoided contact with other tribes, though occasionally conflict arose at imagined borders and overlapping spheres of influence. Mostly these occurred about a favoured swimming point or exceptionally rich rock pool, and ended sharing or with a few verbal exchanges, one tribe departing the scene temporarily and uneasily.

There were great open-air sea baths along the coast replenished on each tide, but these were well supervised and regulated and could not provide the excitement of the untamed coast.

Courting couples and young lovers were also drawn to the coast on those long, hot, summer days or in the evening after work. These adults were strangely preoccupied with each other, unpredictable and only safely observed from a distance. Later in life we would learn more about such things, but in that time tribes of children, beyond adult influence, by the coast, midweek in high summer, reigned supreme. There were no rules, only the pleasure and desires of the tribe, till hunger drove them homewards towards nightfall. Satiated, memories abundant, and anticipation of the next day made for dream-filled sleep.

Over the summers the Bay would reveal daily more of its treasures and mysteries, brought sometimes capriciously, other times stormily by wind and wave, tide and receding tide and currents, drawing from the Irish Sea and Atlantic beyond. Our Bay was linked to the world!

* * *

At some point in summer, the "jellies" or jellyfish, to give them their recognised, full, and incorrect name, being neither jelly nor fish, would appear.

Mysterious and beautiful in the water, floating by or gently trying to propel themselves away from the coast and the shallows where wave and tide threatened to throw them up, to collapse under their own skeletonless, gelatinous mass, desiccate in the sea breeze and sun, and lifelessly fade away. Not even a stain is left in evidence.

Common jellyfish, translucent globes with neon coloured reproductive organs in the outline of a four-leafed shamrock, would appear individually to begin with, followed by hordes, gently with imperceptible sting. Compass jellyfish, their globes marked radially, trailing tentacles, could sweep across swimmers, mooring ropes, and nets, leaving stinging cells even after their departure, reminiscent of brushing nettles. And the Gorgon of this trio was the Lion's Mane with snakelocks suspended from the underside of its mantle, contact with which could paralyse like the Medusa herself. Dublin Bay for some reason was a hot spot for Lion's Mane. There were others and more coming.

Ever wonder, how you'd respond to an alien invasion? Would your humanity withstand the fear of the unknown?

When the first jellyfish would appear, the young tribes along the coast would operate as an early warning system and unite in common defence. Once the first swimmers had been stung, they would counter attack.

Neither knowing nor understanding their perceived enemy, the advance columns of jellyfish would be stoned in the water, before they bellied to land. As the legions bloomed and grew, the deadlier stingers would be the target of the most violent assaults as they beached. The tribes were in killing frenzy, stabbing with sticks and driftwood, stoning and bombing with larger rocks, careful never to make personal contact with these helpless, gelatinous, marooned creatures from the deep. Sometimes a sensitive child, more often than not a girl, might discreetly try to refloat the smaller, more colourful and harmless jellies, resembling as they did costume jewellery and equating pretty with innocent. However, the soldiers, as they now perceived themselves, mostly boys and united across tribes, were taking no prisoners and giving no quarter and the slaughter would continue, till the beaches were again safe for swimmers. Only when the dangers were repelled and life along the coast returned to normality, would the tribes again go their separate ways. The slain were left disfigured and defaced, where they fell, as warning to further invaders, till they, too, faded back to beach. Further invasions would unite them again and be repelled in similar fashion, little realising the "brainless" jellyfish, with only a simple sensory network, were already doomed on land, and environmental triggers gave rise to the sudden blooms and equally sudden disappearances. For the defenders of the coast, it had been their war and their victory.

As adults now, these warriors of the jellyfish wars ask the question whether we or wildlife need to be protected from the wild in the first instance.

Jellies in the Irish Sea and other depleted fisheries around the world may well be blooming in ever greater abundance and have caused the closure of swimming beaches in recent years. Fears have been expressed where fisheries have collapsed due to human excess and recovery may now be difficult or impossible, where jellies hold and occupy the niche. Angel Skate and Electric Ray have disappeared from the Irish Sea and Cod is commercially extinct. Turtles, including the giant Leathery Turtle, the size of a small family car, are also endangered by human excess and waste and come into the Irish Sea to feed on jellyfish, a balance existing since the time of the dinosaurs.

So when the jellies invade in ever greater numbers and become an insuperable force, will the "Lord of the Jellies" and inventor of the "God-machine" respond in killing mode or step back to consider how a quite "brainless" creature could have come so far and where responsibility truly lies? Only in understanding, can we respond!

* * *

Many years ago the Blaschka family in Dresden brought Victorian glass art to its zenith, producing glass jellyfish, anatomically perfect in scale and colour, such was the regard for their beauty. The finest collection of these resides in Dublin's Natural History Museum or the "Dead Zoo," as affectionately known to Dubliners. Later and already a century ago, Maude Delap, a reclusive rector's daughter on Valentia Island off Kerry, with primitive equipment, became the first to breed jellies in bell jars, cracking much mystery of their origins, life cycles, and blooms. It took a century for the patriarchal scientific profession to recognise the achievements of this great, disenfranchised lady.

Have the children of Dublin Bay within us all matured sufficiently to overcome our horror and fear of the unknown and to learn from it?

Further invasions are already underway and the frontline is forever moving.

On mature reflection the question arises: Were jellies the enemy or messengers?

PANDORA'S BOX

*Fadó, Fadó,** many years ago, I met and married a woman called Jack, so named for versatility, and full of stories of rural cottage life from beyond the Pale, the old boundary of British rule and government.

We'd both worked and met in the capital of Ireland and were now part of the flight from the suburbs and city, seeking to recapture that rural idyll and we found a home, *Clochán,** close to her place of birth, just inside that old Pale boundary.

Jack had childhood memories of beating away hunting hounds in her garden with brooms in defence of a cornered and fleeing stag, so we put up signs around our new acre forbidding hunters in that most intensively hunted part of Ireland. Neither stag or fox nor hare would be hunted across this acre and could have refuge there.

There were good neighbours all round, notwithstanding their hunt traditions, and so we were good-humouredly welcomed as oddities. With development, the area is not much different to the suburbs now, but rural traditions, including the hunt, persist. Represented by Rural Ireland,* they are on the back foot now, as we were many years previous. Such debates oscillate endlessly, favouring reformers for a while, and then reverting to traditionalists, inching toward change over centuries rather than years.

I remember, on arrival in the area, an old one-eyed friend and neighbour advising me against sheep for keeping grass down, on the premise it was cattle and tillage country and I followed his advice, as on many occasions after, I was grateful to do.

Our place, however, was to be sanctuary to all, from jackdaws to criminals, and the course of our lives for time to come was set.

In time, with European subsidies, even the sheep came in. How things change over a lifetime!

Much of the hedgerows and field boundaries, however, remain, still refuge to rabbit, hare, fox, badger, and even outlier deer, and argument and debate about the pursuit of the uneatable by the unspeakable, still continues energetically in the local pubs. Really, only individuals change and make choices, and wildlife likely will still be there long after we are gone.

As the country flourished, so too did the Irish love affair with the horse. Cattle came back, sheep went into decline, and still the wildlife found refuge in the hedgerows and copses.

Our little sanctuary survives, but with or without it, the hidden and secret casualties of human encroachment and development still find sanctuary in the hearts and homes of individuals they encounter throughout Ireland, even by chance.

One wild and rainy night, a knock came to our door, late, and in the dark and shadows, a great-coated man was sheltering, one arm enclosed in his coat.

"You take rescued animals?" he asked without introduction and, having agreed, he drew a small fox cub, silvery-grey more than red, eyes not yet open, from his great-coat and thrust it gently upon me with the parting words to "mind this and never say where it came from," as he disappeared into the dark.

This little creature, the first of many, was a gift from the area and became an ambassador for us all, ancient residents and blow-ins, like us, alike. The night orphan was to bring many together.

Jack fixed it up with a box for a bed, a water-bottle and undertook the nursing of it, soon to be christened Pandora by her. It wasn't long off the mother,* rescued from hounds at a dig out, traumatised but belly still full, and so she slept well, without further attention, that first night.

The little fox grew fast and unruly as a household pet. Tame and loveable, she was never to be trained.

As her eyes opened, and more household destruction and play on her mind, we moved her out to an old caravan beside some goslings. The next morning we found her attached more by gums than teeth to a gosling as big as herself, and the gosling still gasping for breath. The gosling survived Pandora's best young effort, but it was evident the wild was in her. The instincts were, as should be, untrainable.

It was temporarily back to the house, where she taunted dog and cat alike.

As she grew strong and moved outside, she became more independent and going to sleep at night, we'd often hear late night revellers from the village pubs walking by startled and commenting on the fox about their feet as she followed them. She wandered farther and farther, returning occasionally for food, while remaining friendly and tame. True to her kind, having been part of a human circle, opportunistically she took to robbing groceries from open kitchens and boots from outside doors, and even habitual hunters tolerated and humoured her.

More and more homes were host to Pandora and none wished her harm.

Pandora was a box of tricks, delighting and enchanting all her neighbours to the point shepherds would simply chase her off and hunters undertook to call off hounds if caught on her scent. How realistic that could ever be, how long it could continue, we will never know, as she met her end in the jaws of a great yard-dog whose food dish she tried to rob. She made it home but died of injuries, haemorrhaging internally, responsive to human touch and Jack to the last.

We all learned much about her and the role of her kind in the countryside. Our mistakes in her rearing were to be her downfall, but she became an ambassador for her kind.

Like the fox in Exuperay's* *The Little Prince*, she could be tamed but not trained and the stars and experiences of her, remind us regularly of her passing. On the night of her passing, a new star was born in the heavens.

Still, the hunters follow hounds on the trail of fox, stag, and hare or drag, and still others rear orphans.

The gentleman that rescued Pandora for his young daughter was famous far and wide for his command of hunting dogs and clearing out dens and setts* on farmland, a practise he abandoned after having rescued her.

He is a conservator and wood-turner now and his pieces grace the rooms of royalty. A tree must now fall before it is used. One was even used to present the St. Patrick's Day* shamrock to the US president at the White House in Washington.

Pandora continues to play tricks on us all. And none remembers her more fondly than Jack, who has successfully provided sanctuary for and rehabilitated many wild orphans since, as well as rearing two children and many more rehabilitators.

A "Zoo"
Logical Experience

Work should never get in the way of living, but like every one of my generation, I was to grow up and expected to find gainful employment and a "real job." Landless in Ireland, work with animals was scarce. Animals were for food or industrial production or to serve as beasts of burden and their husbandry and care was to increase output. Even the veterinary profession practised mostly about the meat trade, and there were cattle drives and long lorry and ship voyages to Great Britain, Europe, and North Africa, which only the strongest survived. A group of erstwhile suffragettes brought the live horse trade and much of this cruel live animal trade from Ireland to an end by peaceful protest on the Dublin docks.

Aristocrats and the merchant class would keep horses and hunting dogs, hiring stable hands and labourers to mind them. In this strange and stratified society, there was an ambivalent and distant attitude to animal welfare, in the main delegating the care duties to the hired help. In the "Humanity Dick" Martin* tradition, philanthropic ladies mostly, also addressed themselves to welfare issues among the lower orders of animal and human. The more enlightened merged their efforts.

By and large animals had to work and earn their keep, even the dogs and cats of the country cottages and the new suburbs. They were there to hunt and fetch game, provide security or rodent control, and would rarely see a vet. Racing and wagering on pigeons, dogs, horses, and anything that would compete was another use and these champions and their owners might achieve fame and fortune.

Companionship was always secondary and a bonus.

The options for someone determined to work with animals were few. In this desert there was the "a Zoo" the third oldest zoological society in the world, with a garden of exotic and fearsome beasts from every corner of the earth, and venue for every Holy Communion outing in reach of Dublin city. Alongside Guinness and Nelson's pillar, to be replaced by the spire, it was Dublin's main tourist attraction.

Dublin Zoo was behind high hedges in Phoenix Park, itself the largest enclosed city park in the world and home also to the president of Ireland, in the lesser of two white houses. The greater mind was also designed by an Irishman! To children the zoo was a trip around the world in eighty minutes and a dizzying, mesmeric experience meeting the creatures of myth and legend and story. Funny, most of them did it in a rush, followed by an equally rushed feed of chips and rarely came back till they had children of their own.

I, however, was attracted to it like a moth to a flame and applied year on year, through school and college for work, ultimately securing an apprentice keeper's position after graduation and a succession of "real jobs," breaking family traditions and succession in the zoo itself. Other traditions were broken at that time, with another graduate to follow me the first, and the first female on the keeper staff. There was to be a fusion of old and new and the future looked exciting. My family, and soon to be life partner, all supported me in this madness, drop in pay, and belief in my ability to build a career from this lowly position in this neglected institution.

My first day as a worker rather than a visitor was unforgettable. I was expecting to learn and work to the highest standards of animal husbandry and welfare and be at the cutting edge of wildlife science and conservation. I was to discover elephant's teeth grew forwards all their lives along conveyor lines from the back, fresh ones replacing worn ones at the front, till they ran out. Neither did ducks always "walk and talk like ducks," like the ones familiar to us in the rivers, parks, and canals of the city, rather there were ones that nested in trees and others that whistled rather than quacked. Initially there was much to learn, but soon it was evident society interests had largely replaced zoological ones.

Like Xanadu, these institutions, now more old than venerable, were the pleasure domes of their day. Their fortunes had crumbled with the disintegrating empire and they held little in common with the aristocratic but, at times, great scientific exploration that had accompanied earlier discoveries. Scientists were never well-served by commerce or strident nationalism, and many zoological institutions had become corrupted, their principle purpose putrefied, providing little knowledge yet being responsible for much cruelty. Like the human inmates of Bedlam,* the animal inmates of zoos had become shadows and caricatures of their former selves and their wild counterparts, and were merely drawing crowds of the poor and their pennies to bolster falling income and support the indulgences and addictions of aristocrats to stations in society no longer earned or merited.

"We're in show business," was the quote of a director of the day and "conservation has no place in the zoo's constitution," was the quote of a society president. Science had transformed to showmanship and the travelling shows, wildlife traders, and zoos had all become interlinked, operating a revolving door policy for animals, or trading triangle, as it became known.

Scandals at the zoo became almost daily events.

As society transformed there was renaissance and public enquiry and advances again in science. Conservation replaced entertainment and this endeavour engaged the masses in increasingly novel ways.

Modern zoos, sea worlds, Disney, and biosphere parks have refined these old attractions to be all but unrecognisable from the true wild. Virtual reality replaces reality as the barriers become concealed and inmates revealed. Award-winning wildlife photographers and filmmakers now often produce their winning material from captive collections, a contradiction in itself. Celebrities and artistes adopt and promote captives in name of their wild relations, without a hint of irony. Expanded cages and enclosures are termed habitats and even ecosystems. Arctic and Antarctic species live in refrigerated units in tropical regions; tropical and desert species live in huge biospheres in northerly latitudes and winters; marine creatures and even whales live in land-locked tanks and these are viewed as natural and naturalised! And so the wild is brought to the great urban conurbations, close to airports, motor and rail access, and the illusion for all but the most enlightened is complete. Some of these institutions even call themselves sanctuaries, protecting wildlife from the wild! And to these institutions worldwide, masses of people flock, the huge merchandising and retailing outlets associated with them, relieving them of their pennies, directly competing with simple nature for attention and resources. The operation is painless and the revenue and resource disparities so disproportionate as to leave the damaged wild directly threatened and the merchants prospering on identity theft and illusion.

Not so different yet to my first day in a famous city zoo, many years ago, or indeed even to predecessors of mine a century and a half previous!

Confronted with the sounds, smells, and testosterone of the place, immersed in its history and folklore, awed by the keepers of these great, exotic, strange, and wonderful animals, dominion was confused with care and dependency with appreciation. Novice keepers even today and worldwide, meeting the world's wild cats, great and small, behind solid iron bars on wooden benches in Victoriana or glass in the new cities; The Big (and famed) Five of Africa; marsupials of the southern hemisphere; primates watching your every move and mistake; creatures of the Arctic and Antarctic,

New world and Old, land sea and air, all collected together in menagerie and within arm's reach, are overwhelmed. The cloying and clinging smell of freshly slaughtered meat and old blood about the predators' cages sustaining their unbroken frenzy; the warm comforting smell of the herbivore houses; the ammonia of the aviaries; and the heat and humidity among the obese reptiles suffused the senses. So strong was the sensory infusion and brainwashing that it was akin to narcotic-induced acceptance of the illusion and denial of the realities of cruelty and suffering.

I was bewitched and it took many years and many casualties to impress on me, however clever and scientific and caring, we become, we can take the animal out of the wild but not the wild out of the animal, no more than the bog out of the bogman, and by trying to do so, we more often than not do great and cruel disservice to fellow creatures and their conservation.

I walked through those Victorian gates to work with the animals of the ark, in the footsteps of giants, and the belief I would be contributing to advances in the science and welfare of these animals in my care. It took death, injury, and insanity among the inmates to stir me, and the instruction and leadership of older and more enlightened keepers than I to challenge the crippling system.

Many men had become brutalised by the institution they signed to serve, and with old-school ties they combined to fiercely resist change.

I was lucky! There was a poet, a gigolo, a smart philosopher, stones in place of rocks, and a bishop to start a humble revolution. These men, in oral tradition in the tea rooms of the zoo, had kept true to stories, memories, and historical fact to feed a rebellion and direct it. Their tales have yet to be recorded but are essential to ongoing reform. These remain unfinished business until their role is acknowledged in what followed, as the most transforming decade of the zoo's entire two-century history with follow on effects worldwide. It was the letting in of the light! *Sin scéal eile, le leabhar eile!*

The death of Judy, a young African elephant, was to become the spark and the intervention of a kindly, reforming vet from England who could not accept the growth of science at the expense of beauty. London Zoo, simultaneously, was facing similar scandal and crisis, giving rise to the Born Free Foundation.*

I was to lose my job for simply doing my "real job" and bringing these together. The years of isolation and injustice to follow gave rise to a tide of public opinion, demanding better conditions for animals and resulting in a government enquiry. This was convened by a controversial *Taoiseach** of the day and chaired by a legendary, straight-talking national rugby player, coach and vet.

The report was damning of the "a Zoo" conditions and practises, so much so a subsequent *Taoiseach* recommissioned it for public consumption. With the passage of time, archivists and historians will revisit much of that period of unfinished business and learn from it.

The age-old city hall and Irish solution of throwing money at the problem followed and, under new management, some transparency and public debate.

I was vindicated but never forgiven. This most transforming period in the zoo's history and the plight of the animals had gripped the nation and fuelled a public debate that resulted in a review, personally and nationally, of our relations with wildlife. Much unlearning had to be done and the patently obvious lesson that no good could come of cruelty and denial is still being learned.

Eden, with all its wonderful and exotic representatives of the wildlife kingdom, imploded first, and then exploded across Dublin city, releasing new ideas and new energy. Dubliners may well be the most zoo-literate city population in the world today, and none better for engaging the world in this ongoing renaissance. It is a delicate process requiring careful nurturing by zoo managers, scientists, and conservationists, and they must take courageous steps to eliminate systemic cruelties in the trade and institutions. Redemption demands honesty and they need to encourage, question, and challenge their keepers. The public retains right of engagement. The genie is out of the bottle and cruelty does not serve or represent our wishes or interests as a species.

I left a changed man. For me there was no going back, and I'd be led by the animals and children thereafter. It was new territory and I was open to new thinking and experience, and hope the zoos are also. After a decade, there was never a view of the "a Zoo" as good as the one from the road leaving and looking back!

I remain mindful that wildlife remains gravely threatened and nature protection vastly under-resourced, and many gifted and passionate young animal handlers still take the road I did to work with animals. I was just one, and one of the few to escape. Many remain within these institutions trying to reform them and extend into field programmes, rehabilitation, and education. Many still become brutalised, defending unquestioningly the institutions and systemic failures within them.

From the Colosseum to the menagerie, and travelling shows to modern zoos, the issues and principles under debate have remained the same over the centuries. Only the scale and reach has changed and it must be facilitated, not hijacked by market-speak or censored, if the institutions and ourselves are not to become evolutionary full-stops.

If Gandhi is right and a society may be measured by its treatment of the most vulnerable and animals, then we all have much to measure against.

GRACED BY GREY SEALS

I've journeyed alongside this species for more than a quarter of a century and unashamedly confess to an attachment to them, rivalling that of family and friends. And no, I am not and never have been anthropomorphic and this in no way devalues my family and friends, who also living alongside the "enchanted people," as many know the seals, came to regard them as extended family. As the Irish Seal Sanctuary* grew in our home and garden, so, too, did our horizons and world expand. Those three words—Irish Seal Sanctuary—summed up everything we did and the whole of our existence for more than a quarter century, and we shared the experience with everyone who wanted. None were refused. People from all around the coast brought the seals to us, and it was not for us to refuse or demur.

For many of us coast-wide, simple gut responses to the plight of orphaned, injured, or simply sick seals on beaches evolved into greater understanding and a search for further understanding of our natural world and the relationships and dependencies between land and sea. Seals turned our earth on its head, making us realise often "land divided, where sea united."

In wildlife rehabilitation we understood so little, we let the seals lead us, aided by what little scientific and veterinary advice was available, and pro bono masters of their science and art came to

32

help us. Doors opened for the seals on the premise wildlife need not pay. For all of us, it became a journey to the heart of the natural world and all that impacted it. We drew from folklore, science, fisheries, and the knowledge and experience of coast-dwellers and communities, but mostly from the seals themselves. We were being taught.

Rescue was easy! Sanctuary was as natural as home-cooking! Release was the objective and everybody helped, turning out in record numbers on beaches, never before seen for wildlife events. Rehabilitation was the word we knew so little about, and then the understanding came; it was as much about our rehabilitation as it was the seal's.

What brought these animals to us? How could we rehabilitate a creature, the result of millennia of evolution, from such a poorly understood and unexplored realm? The marine institute had resources and ships. The Irish Seal Sanctuary had people and we were all in the flippered hands of the enchanted people and led by them as we tried to assist them, independence and integrity intact, back to their realm.

Over a quarter century and almost a thousand seals, I struggled with them and my own ignorance, cursed them many a winter's night and wished them someplace else … anywhere else but on my patch and my watch. But that was the hand I was dealt in life, which for many of us, as often as not, is a series of accidents more than plan! Fish-breathing, foul-smelling, bad-mouthed, often cantankerous impostors of much more alluring infants, who'd bite the hand that feeds as quick as look at it—these were to become my constant working companions. They have got me in endless trouble from the time of our engagement, but I wouldn't have changed anything or for anything, so much have I learned and experienced. I've been shown the coast of Ireland, unseen to tourists, taken to sea by fishermen, and have access to political leaders and ambassadors on their behalf.

The Irish Seal Sanctuary exists to share seal knowledge and wisdom with all. Intermediaries, as they are between land and sea, the enchanted people have much to teach us and, in a quirky way, if you are open to it, help us more than we help them. The Irish Seal Sanctuary merely provides an under-resourced halfway house and sanctuary. The volunteers that have given their lives, or time out of their lives, are there to make sense with you of the many messages the seals bring.

Humanity, no less than individuals, had no great plan to destroy the earth, but by greed, ignorance, and a series of unplanned accidents is doing quite a good job of just that. The prospect of disinheriting our children may wake us all too late! Such as the seals and those who speak for them are messengers now.

Grey seals became the world's first species protected by legislation a hundred years ago, just as the world's first national parks were also emerging. Wildlife and wilderness were acquiring rights and had champions, in an age of enlightenment that was abolishing slavery, bringing the vote to women, and democracy to nations. Sanctuaries apart, for wildlife rights, progress was slow, unable to defend itself in the face of industrialisation and globalisation, and moved little beyond the dream. Where did it all stop? When did we forget? Most recently, in a first time ever initiative, Bolivia is according rights to Earth. Is this a step we should follow on our journey back to the future?

Seals have always been centre-stage to every international debate relating to wildlife conflict, sustainable development, wise-use strategies, and calls for culls. They are vilified by the more archaic sectors of the fishing industry. They are the first species threatened with mass extinction by climate change. Harbingers of famine at sea, fish-stock collapses, victims of ocean debris, bye-catch and pollution, confronting, understanding, and resolving their issues becomes key to resolving our own problems and path to a more sustainable future for next generation, our children.

Seals are the most efficient and economic indicators of the health of fish stocks and biodiversity. They are canaries for climate change. They are the foundation and pillar to the growing, sustainable marine ecotourism industry.

They are entitled to live as they have always lived, according to their own lights and rights and as we intrude into their realm, it is for us to reach harmonious accommodation with them. A seal passing through our sanctuary is much like a beloved, eccentric, wandering relation who turns up for family occasions with stories to tell.

Need I be more scientific, or can you accept the testimony of a life graced by grey seals?

Future generations of Irish Seal Sanctuary rehabilitators may be more scientific, but mind and heart must remain open to grace if more is to be learned. Rehabilitators of many species and animals worldwide provide this opportunity for engagement and grace, as do guides into the natural world.

My children grew up in a garden full of seals. My family and I are among the lucky ones! Without the support of family and friends, this journey with seals could not have happened for me. Many shared that experience with us and it is the task of the Irish Seal Sanctuary to continue to share it with others.

Mountjoy

One day I received a phone call from a teacher enquiring after wildlife talk and a guest speaker for her class.

Her class was in a prison, a far cry from the usual school and college talks I would give on wildlife, second chances for wildlife casualties, and assisting wildlife back to freedom and independence.

What would these, men mostly, want to know about wildlife and how difficult would the subject of freedom be for them, incarcerated for whatever crimes, without privilege or even vote, their every minute of every day, regulated by guards?

To a wildlife rehabilitator, their position is anathema and the most unimaginable and horrific situation in which any living thing could find itself.

Difficult for them! I was really thinking how difficult it would be for me!

The teacher was friendly, persuasive, and passionate that her pupils be denied no more than the minimum proscribed by law and relevant to their crimes. Education and opportunity for rehabilitation was at the very least their right and prejudice, resources, and the great walls, bars, doors and locks would not deny it them, if she had any say. In her class, in their minds and imaginings, they would at least be free.

I was entirely under her spell and not knowing exactly how I'd cope, I agreed. I was to discover how under-resourced education and rehabilitation really were and how hard these teachers had to fight for their classes. How could anyone say no to such an invitation?

Mountjoy was probably the most inappropriately named building in Dublin City. Those inside could not see out nor those outside see in, beyond those tall brooding walls. Much of it ageing and derelict, the walls screamed out with the pain and horror of lives destroyed and even lost within. It accommodated, if that word can even be used, the criminals of the city in the most appalling and overcrowded conditions, earning it its Dickensian reputation as the most penal and punitive of all such institutions in Europe. So solid were its walls, no sound even escaped.

The city was blissfully unaware of the population within, dismissing even mention of them, as having put themselves above the law, and so the law put them beyond, where they could do no further harm or injury to others. Wasn't that rather simple? I was to realise the teachers unflinchingly believed in their pupils and the power of education to help them rehabilitate and return to society. And should this not also be a priority of prison? The reality says not and these teachers struggle for rights as concessions. Monolithic like Ayers Rock or the pyramids, these appeals were entombed within.

On the appointed day, I approached the great gates of the prison and was led through a little door within. Accompanied by the teacher, I was screened, and then taken through successive locked gates to a bustling interior of cells, galleries, and common space. In a small alcove was the "Auld Triangle" famed of song and story and rung to assemble prisoners. It was not unlike the bell in a school yard.

All eyes followed every movement and event, and all were under surveillance all the time. It felt nothing or nobody relaxed but were perpetually in a heightened state of anticipation.

To my surprise, and I was to do more after that, I found the talks easy and informal and the men enjoyable and informative. I say men always, as they are the majority population in prisons and I had only all-male classes. They were mostly young men and they were eager to contribute, discuss, and engage, and to be able to do so freely, as their teacher rightly insisted.

They were mostly of city background and many grew up around dogs, cats, and the famous Dublin urban horses. Some came from farming and fishing backgrounds.

All encountered wildlife at some point in their lives, and so I was learning the reach of wildlife into their lives as much as they were learning from me.

In that barren place, through memories of wildlife we were sharing, as sure as the air we breathe, the water we drink, and the sun, the moon and the stars looking down on us. We had more in common on this earth than the walls that divided us. I think often of those men and wonder how they are now. I hope they are, again, out walking dogs, crossing fields on foot or horseback, or on the sea and free!

* * *

On a particular occasion, I was asked to visit the male AIDS wing. In those panicked and uninformed days, the AIDS prisoners were kept separate from the general population. As a virtual recluse, working in wildlife rehabilitation, I knew little of the ungrounded paranoia and fear surrounding AIDS at the time, and so was glad to do as asked. I did not understand the fuss and appreciation expressed when I said yes, and remain humbled by the memory of it since. These were "brothers lepered," and some authority had made an added crime of their sickness.

When I came to visit, a boisterous group of about a dozen young, strong men were finishing their lunch of sausage, beans, and mash, and returning plates. They came from a small, steaming kitchen, still smelling of the meal and grease, into a small adjoining room, barely big enough to seat them and with room for me at the head of their class. The paint was peeling off the walls in this poorly lit windowless room.

My twelve solid men settled in, after some banter, making use of what little leg room they had to recline and relax.

Other than a sideways look, they ignored me till I addressed them and then fixedly, collectively, and humorously turned their stare on me, as if to say "now entertain us."

I'd planned to show some slides of whales using an old projector on one of the bleak, peeling walls, and so off we went on an imaginary whale-watching trip. First up was a picture of a blue whale, as alien to me, I must say, as any of them, never having seen more than a skeleton in the "Dead Zoo," another wonderful relic of Victorian Dublin, or the Natural History Museum, to give it its proper name. Those of us who ran the city streets as children were familiar with such places.

As I was trying to wax eloquent about a creature, with whose aged, aerially strung, beached skeleton I only had familiarity with, I spied or thought I did the far more familiar, whiskered face of a tiny white mouse emerging from the open-necked collar of a cotton shirt, adorning one of my laid-back pupils in the front seats. It disappeared as quickly as it had appeared. Had I really seen it in the first place? But I had blinked and my delivery was broken, and I was only met again with that wall of friendly fixed stares bemused at my confusion.

The familiar among the unfamiliar! Momentarily, I put it down to my imaginings in this cauldron of pent-up physical and mental energy and resumed my flow, about humpback whales now, equally unfamiliar to me, and didn't the more familiar rodent face appear again from the other side of my attentive pupil's collar. It had definite pink eyes.

Familiarity certainly can breed content and I was laughing to myself to the apparent bemusement of my attentive listeners. I looked around this fine band of young men I could so easily imagine out on a building site or football field—and a more attentive class you could not have wished for—their stares, increasingly mischievous, dared me to give voice to the evidence of my eyes or continue. So continue I did, and didn't the little rodent peep out again and another one from the collar of the lad next to him.

I could not contain the laughter any longer and after initial mock denials, whales were forgotten for that day and instead they shared their stories with me about their pets inside and their experiences with animals in a previous life.

I was sad to leave those men that day. They had taken me on a journey of innocence and discovery. They were not big name criminals. For the most part, their biggest crime was poverty, missed education, learning difficulties, social exclusion, drug dependency, and just taking a wrong turn, like so many of us have done but never had to pay for. There are few more self-educated populations than prisoners and seamen through radio and reading, and their teachers fight an uphill battle to have them recognised and afforded second chances.

As I took leave, I was conscious they could not follow and when I stepped back on the city footpaths, I was so glad, I ran as fast as my legs could drive me, gulping huge lungfuls of free air, my thoughts screaming freedom.

I was only in there for one hour.

THE REFUGEE CUB

It was a muggy autumn day, ground muddy underfoot, and I went for a walk with Jody, down the fields behind my home.

The fields were small, rough grazing, thick hedgerows in berry now. Blackberry, haws, elder, and rosehips, home to badger, fox, rabbits, a wonderland of smell and scent, and track for any young hunter, predator, or inquisitive cub.

I walked and followed while she led, her motion and markings blending her perfectly in with the baring growth and falling leaves, signalling winter and hunger to follow, the great crop, and harvest of wild food.

She was growing strong and fit and exploring the new world, not yet hers, in pursuit of prey yet to be caught.

A distant folk memory drove her to explore, scent, stalk, and follow.

This was a huntress in the making, bred so far from her ancestors, in a distant and strange land. It was already obvious that no hunter like her ever before stalked these small fields.

As we crossed ditches already saturated with the oncoming rains, I became mesmerised.

And so the next few hours passed, as we crossed field on field from the town land of Tobergregan to Ballymadun, with never the sight of anticipated quarry, but always expecting.

Birds had the good sense to stay high in the bushes or the air. Pheasants crashed out of the undergrowth, clapping wings, as out of cannon on a trajectory fleeing the unfamiliar approaching predator. Even for the cub predator, such prey was incidental and a distraction.

She was tiring now but undaunted, and so the decision to turn home had to be mine. I became the quarry, engaging in her cub games later to become lethal, to entice her home.

This cub was her own master, would never bend to human will, and only humoured her carers.

It was enough to call her name and flee homewards, zigzagging all the way. Each time the cub chased, sprang, and felled me and I'd have to surrender, laying side-by-side, rubbing through her magnificent fur in submission and praise, and she would again lick the hand that fed her in affection after months of nursing. These were her rules, not mine and yard-by-yard, field-by-field, we'd repeat the routine until we were both back at her pen, where water, food, and rest in a straw bed awaited.

Only four months old now, her potential was astounding.

I left her to rest for the afternoon and walked the same fields again myself after lunch. Alone, I was not fractionally as alert or sensitised to the life around me and was enjoying a far more leisurely and less exhausting walk, picking my way slowly and much less deliberately among the poorly managed fields, a simple shadow on the landscape of those hunters who walked before me.

A pack of hounds in disarray with whipper-ins going wild distracted me from the daydream and reverie of my private thoughts.

From the vantage point of a five-barred gate, I could see a pack of harrier hounds in disarray chasing scent the way I walked earlier.

This normally obedient, disciplined pack of powerful hunters were running in every direction, to the frustration of their handlers. One of the handlers approached me, enquiring the direction of some of the dogs and wholly confused at their unwillingness to respond to command.

I could only smile, confess ignorance, and leave them to the task of rounding up their unhinged hounds. Some, I believe, took days to recover and the story of the ruined hunt remains a mystery to this day. Somewhere a relieved hare was also safe for another day.

I looked in on Jody's pen on my way home and she was contentedly sleeping in her straw after her feed.

Jody was a four-month Siberian-x-something tiger cub, lost in an alien land far from home, the progeny of irresponsible breeding and illegal wildlife trade. Later this refugee cub, the concern she generated, and the controversy she created, was to become the reason for Ireland's final ratification of the United Nations Convention for International Trade in Endangered Species. The minister, who signed off and released Jody's passport to allow her to travel to an American sanctuary, became the president of Ireland, and Jody now resides in Wildlife Waystation, Tujunga Canyons in California, living out her days.

The fields of Tobergregan, Garristown, Ireland still harbour her scent ... that of the world's largest cat.

Footprints in the Snow

While sanctuary was evolving about me, my own career had become kaleidoscopic and catastrophic. From farms to the national zoo, I had become merely a gaoler to many animals and species from all parts of the world. I was soon to discover levels of husbandry at the zoo were lower and freedoms less than on the farms of the day.

In the emerging struggle with the authorities of this Victorian institution, I was daily conflicted in my duties of care to these incarcerated animals and the aspirations of welfare, conservation, and ultimately rehabilitation and release.

Many animals suffered and died on my watch in those difficult angst-driven days. Judy, Julie, and Debbie, the teenage elephants; Gilbert the hippo with ingrown tusk; Tommy the raunchy zebra stallion; Adam the wheezy orangutan; Tommy the crocodile; Spunky and Ootek, the polar bears; Yinka and Gori, the mismatched gorillas; lions, tigers, wallabies, and much more.

A great national debate stormed about our stewardship. There were mass meetings of the Royal Zoological Society of Ireland and ultimately a zoo enquiry, forerunner to many national enquiries to follow.

For my efforts to bring this about, my pedigree was challenged, and others with me, as I struggled to come to terms with stewardship of the world's most exotic species. On the outside there was clamour and demand for protection of Irish wildlife, which, as a nation, we were also failing dismally. Protests about the exotics incarcerated for entertainment in the capital city reached their peak.

Orphaned and injured native seals became the lightning rod for my introduction to rehabilitation and I failed those first individuals miserably.

As I and the national zoo drifted apart, dismally at first, later dramatically with my own dismissal and the aforementioned government enquiry, the plight of incarcerated animals finally came to the attention of the courts of the land in ground-breaking cases about elephants, tigers, bears, and others.

Disgraced initially but later vindicated, I turned my attentions to wildlife welfare and the annual storm-driven orphans of the seal-birthing season around our coast, founding the Irish Seal Sanctuary with my wife and others in the process. This grew quickly over the years and we all embarked on an endless journey of discovery. The word sanctuary acted as a magnet, attracting everything from jackdaws to criminals and all in between. This had a life all of its own and many to recount stories of it. Later we'd learn to deal with oiled birds, whaling issues, fishing, and myriad other impacts and threats to wildlife.

For me, the day of realisation came one morning while treating some pox-ridden seal pups from Torai Island* at my home place. For respite I went for a walk in the snow-covered fields with a little refugee tiger cub, called Jody.

She was slowly recovering from pleurisy, rickets, and general deprivation—a victim of the wildlife trade. She was full of the will to live and explore.

As we walked down a country lane, I looked behind to see tiger pads in the snow and instantly knew, though they'd be erased the next day, that I was witnessing something no other Irish person could hope to see, unless it was shared. This refugee cub was to become my animal guide to wildlife rehabilitation.

From there the seals, tigers, and many other animals were to lead me and others on a new learning curve. Our protocols had to be rewritten.

As many rehabilitators to follow were to learn, wildlife had not read our books. With the dictum "let the animal lead you," rehabilitation became animal-centred. The animals were with us merely for respite, recovery, temporary sanctuary, and ultimately release, freedom being the greatest gift to any wild thing.

Freedom to what? Habitats that would no longer sustain them, so severely have we impacted them! And so, the frontline of the battle for wildlife becomes a battle for our mutual survival and sanctuary is our immediate response.

As we were to learn from footprints in the snow, sanctuary can be but a staging post to full recovery and freedom.

Thanks to our tinkering Jody is an evolutionary full stop, living out her days at a California Waystation, and our challenge remain to rebuild bridge-heads to independent living for wildlife.

Those footprints are long erased and the journey is only underway. Another generation will build on our efforts.

The Princess
and the Ellies

I was anticipating a quiet day—routine reconnaissance of a circus—travelling with three adult, female Asian elephants and a young, pubescent African bull elephant. Word was, these animals were, as many of their kind in the alien travelling shows of this part of the world, shackled fore and aft and grossly underweight.

I had earlier wagered in the free press that these four elephants were collectively fifteen hundred imperial pounds underweight, with an Irish punt for every imperial pound, I was out to a charity of the show people's choice. As show people would normally respond to a wager, I hoped they would bring the elephants to a weighbridge, but no! I was probably on the button.*

Emaciation in circus elephants is rarely evident to the customers who see them in pomp and panoply, regalia and spotlight, performing for less than an hour a day in the ring. Circuses are an ancient tradition, bespeaking our dominion over beast and control of them. The elephant trainer is owner and master of the great muscled mammoths, bending their will to perform acts for our entertainment and minuscule reward.

This dominion and mastery is dressed as benevolence to the beasts, further heightening our sense of superiority over the creatures, and children are allowed to present them titbits and climb over them after the performance. The new age mastodons are

47

appreciative of the break in their day and the momentary kindness of children.

Before the performance I was going to inspect these particular elephants, incognito, with my little daughter, the "golden princess," all of four years old.

She was dressed for the day in a padded, purple, favourite coat and woolly hat, unwitting accessory to my routine investigation, and her excitement and anticipation for a day at the circus was infectious to me. The joy of a day out with my beautiful daughter, little hand in mine, pulling ahead all the time, shaded the more serious nature of my business and transported me to that happy place of childhood faith. We were just going to meet the Ellies.

Entering the circus grounds, we made our way unnoticed to the elephants' tent, a simple covering of tarpaulin over poles, secured by pegs, driven thousands of times by circus roustabouts, as they travelled town to town, country to country, show to show. The elephants endlessly travelling in beast wagons between shows, performed their limited repertoire for an hour a day. When not in the dark wagons or performing, they were in the tent, always shackled left to right or right to left, hind to fore to a wooden floor, with only enough chain to advance a pace to eat or retreat a pace to dung.

An aged and ageless mahogany Indian gentleman, with long grey hair and beard, barely covered himself, sat reclining backwards at the entrance to the tent. He appeared asleep—almost dead—and we passed with a simple acknowledgement.

The interior of the tent provided little protection from the outside temperature or night time chill, and was bathed in the amber light of the sun, falling through the tarpaulin. No Indian or African sun here and just a blow heater to take the chill off the air. The smell was comforting.

And there they were! Back home in their dreamtime, and we were immediately humbled in their presence, shadows though they were, of their wild relations which neither I nor the princess had ever met or seen.

Silent hulks on great pillars of legs, making grey beautiful, skin stretched over their great domed heads and depressed temporal lobes and corrugated about their great skeletons, cascading in folds from their pot-bellies, down the lines of their legs, and hanging loose about the joints.

They were like soldiers on parade, all pointing forward to attention.

As we approached to inspect the guard, they became quietly agitated at the new presence in the tent and glee of a child. The three female Asians began to weave in symphony, rumbling a little, with trunks sashaying forwards and back.

Now we were the centre of attention, while the Indian continued to doze.

Distractedly they fidgeted with remaining wisps of hay, and I was overcome with sadness at their inability to engage beyond their chains. I was shaded now by my daughter's awe and respect, as she wordlessly engaged. We were all enveloped in silent communication, with the child, the lightning rod. Understanding was growing with not a word spoken. The tent felt as though it was exploding with effort to communicate and empathy was breaking the chains and alienation. The cowled piglet eyes were mirror to great hearts and some gentle tactile exchange, trunk to hand ensued. We were all at ease and peace and in harmony.

Finally we came to the young African bull at the end of the line, more exercised and frustrated than the rest.

As the princess reached to meet the extended trunk of the "beast", in a nanosecond he coiled his trunk about her outstretched hand to pull her in. Only the heavens could have directed my next action, having unwittingly exposed my favourite daughter to danger and quicker than time in reverse, I unzipped her favourite coat, pulling her from the sleeves, as the little enraged bull drew the coat back under his fore feet. We watched as he stood on it and ground head and tusks into it, and then calmly retrieved it.

The Indian still slept as we stood in respect before the enraged little bull, all two tonne of him and growing tusks to match. I feigned calm, though my every nerve end was quivering and the blood had drained from my face, smiled at my fearless daughter, and helped her back into her coat.

As we left the tent, passed the sleeping fakir hand-in-hand and emerged back into weak sunlight and cold day, I could hear her chuckling.

"The Elly just wanted to say hello, Daddy," she said to me and, as I hugged her, I could feel great tears welling up inside me and could simply respond between laughter and tears that, indeed, the Elly said hello. The rest of the day was a blur, but we had a great time together and she a great tale to tell her brother and mother.

To this day, my daughter has been muse and nemesis to me many times. She remains fearless and a champion of freedoms for all species, more latterly humans.

My report was irrelevant, as my daughter, strong in mind and body, provides greater testimony and advocacy for freedoms than my life's work ever could. My heroine for human rights remains that four-year-old girl child, and young African elephants belong free in Africa, as should all circus wildlife be returned to their home place!

The princess, I hope, would approve.

Ros Muc* Mons(h)ter

"Have we *monshters* in Ireland?" So went the midnight query, a demand as much as question, one summer from a Ros Muc gentleman.

A reveller in the local pub, he had just exited at midnight to navigate his way home, to be bustled to one side by a mini-monster in his first faltering steps homeward.

His voice on the borrowed phone, faltering a little like his steps, was, however, strong. Querulously, he was fighting back the alcoholic haze, the cynics emerging behind him from the soporific lantern-lit room, peering into the moonlit night in the general direction he was pointing, as the rear of the *monshter* disappeared over a bank, merging ripplelessly into mirror-calm water of the loch and emerging briefly on a small islet just off shore, to be absorbed by the night and hummocks of other rocks.

To the revellers, every rock was now a *monshter* and as they failed to move again for the waiting, watching patrons of the Ros Muc Inn, now all assembled and locked outside the pub, they started to drift home.

My midnight caller, puzzled now, bade me good night politely and ended the phone call. I could only imagine from the other side of Ireland what had happened.

My first caller, Tom Beag,* as he was locally known, a monster of a man himself, known for his work prowess on land and water, was to stick by his story, as more and more came to validate over coming weeks.

Word of the Ros Muc *Monshter* was spreading and being picked up by local and national media. I was intrigued and waited eagerly for my now regular late night calls from Ros Muc. For how often do you get to track, even over the phone, a *monshter*, with the prospect some day of a clearer sighting?

Tom and his neighbours were fast becoming experienced *monshter* sleuths, collecting anecdotal evidence, seeking spoor and track evidence, deploying watchers, but no closer encounter than Tom's first was to be had.

The dustbins out back of the pub would be overturned noisily, with the revellers inside. Patrons would rush to the door to see no more than the now familiar disappearing rump of the beast returning to its offshore islet. Always it was closing time and midnight.

The story spread and was always consistent. Comparisons were drawn with local wildlife, but none matched. The creature was four-legged, shuffled like a badger, snouted gates open like a pig, nocturnal, terrestrial, and aquatic. It was obviously of high intelligence, foraging bins under the noses of pub patrons, using music nights for distraction, and shadows for concealment like a black cat in a dark, windowless room, eluding followers by taking to water.

While the *monshter* descriptions remained consistent and small, its reputation was growing. When local cats, coincidentally or otherwise, went missing, it was elevated to hall of fame status, alongside Nessie, of the loch of the same name in Scotland. When it was reported there had been earth movements on the local football pitch prior to the sightings, associations were made with the spirit world.

Ros Muc is a wonderful weave of land, rock, water, and sea, moved by tide and seasons, never the same and never fully mapped. Cartographers go there and never return. Some are found long-bearded, grey, and old, still working on the same area a lifetime later.

The creature knew this landscape and seascape, knew the light and the shadows, knew when dark drove out light, and was a master of concealment.

In this world there are still faeries and sprites of land and water. Local people respect their sacred places and would never disturb them. Whatever the land produces or sea provides, a portion is left for these spirits of nature to provide for a further season. If these cycles are broken, turbulence and chaos follow and appeasement becomes necessary.

The innkeeper began to leave offerings by the dustbins in hope of a closer sighting, as much as appeasement. The elusive creature availed, but provided no closer contact.

A cosy, comfortable accommodation had arrived, whereby *monshter* and patrons of the Ros Muc Inn led their parallel lives. It was an easy existence, where offerings and foraging apart, neither intruded on the other. The chase was off and the *monshter* would reveal itself, if it willed.

Customers of the inn would simply ask, "Has the *monshter* been by lately?" And, if by chance a visitor to the area overheard and enquired, it would make for a good story and a few free pints. Some blurred, dark photos appeared on the walls of the inn—some allegedly showing aura—and these would be alluded to.

One night a blow-in from another land, living some miles off, was sampling the local hospitality of the Ros Muc Inn and happened to hear the story. He was an exotic pet collector and described an escapee male racoon he had lost weeks prior to first sighting of the *monshter*. His story was listened to politely and courteously, as all guests are treated. Everybody agreed to keep a watchful eye but none, Tom Beag most fervently of all, could confirm any likeness to the local Ros Muc *Monshter*. It was something else entirely, and for many years after and to this day the creature avails of the offerings of the Ros Muc Inn, never fully revealing itself or its lair by day, and continues to stand in great affection of the local people and awe of visitors.

Of course, no racoon or remains have ever been found and the last confirmed sighting was only a few years back, by two equally inebriated revellers.

Everyone knows *monshters* do not die!

Irish Molly

I don't quite remember when I first heard of Molly, a mature little lady bear, former dancer, and performer with a travelling circus, who was retired and leading a life of solitude, removed from her own kind, in a cage in a quarry, outside Limerick, in the West of Ireland.

"Heaven knows no greater rage than a robin redbreast in a cage," were the lines that sprang to mind. How sad, the thought of a bear in one.

Molly was almost an afterthought only coming to attention in a ground-breaking, high profile cruelty and custody case to rescue some tigers, holding that part of the country and the national authorities in perpetual fear of a misadventure.

Bears have had a most troubled and violent relationship with man. From earliest history they competed for the same resources of food and caves for shelter, and the competition was more equal, till fire gave man the advantage. As man settled and kept livestock, they may occasionally have preyed on flocks and herds. They were seen as an intelligent and formidable adversary of man from the earliest times. Maybe the fact they could stand upright on their hind legs and slug it out at eye level in mortal combat gave them their mythological status.

But the relationship corrupted when humans sought to subjugate

them as an expression of their power and civilising influence. For
the bears, this has long been a relationship based on ignominy and
disgrace. They were baited and fought, bear to bull, bear to dogs,
on foot, from horseback, and chased by hounds for reasons mostly
unknown to even their tormentors. Captives were "trained" to perform and dance, and at all times to be subservient. They were
shackled and chained when abroad and about. Often teeth and
claws were pulled.

Bears are escape artists and can run, climb, dig, and swim, and
even open a simple lock, so they were kept in the most primitive
form of captivity known to man—the pit! In the emperor's collection in Austria, they can still be seen, sixty feet down, their only
view of the outside world being the hole to the sky above and gawk-
ing visitors looking down.

Molly's origins were a bit obscure. She was certainly North
American, as Europe's bears are rather scarce after the centuries of
persecution. She was undoubtedly born in captivity in Europe in
the back of a beast wagon or some menagerie. She travelled with a
circus and learned a limited repertoire. You'd only have to whistle
or hum "The Blue Danube Waltz" and she'd start to dance. She
could actually dance better than me.

However, travelling shows touring the same circuit year after year
have to refresh their acts or the crowds complain. "Bums on seats,"
is what show business is all about, and when the bears and big cats
exhaust their repertoire, they are replaced by oncoming new cubs
in training. After a life of entertaining they "disappear" or are
retired to breed another class, often in the most squalid conditions.
It's not so long ago that the corpse of a bear floated down the River
Liffey and into Dublin city. Breeders are effectively farmed. Molly
ended up in such a menagerie.

The place and the owner had come to national attention for the
presence of tigers kept there in squalid and unsafe conditions. There
were also baboons, and all this in the middle of quiet dairy land.

The owner was not a cruel man but victim of his fetish and loyalty to the circus. He was distressed and under siege and a wonderful and humane Garda sergeant removed his gun for safe-keeping. He could not provide adequately, but was unwilling to part and breaking no licensing laws. Eventually the family supported and assisted the rescue and, one would hope, they, too, were relieved of a great burden.

The national society for the protection of all animals had drafted me on to their council to address this growing problem of exotic and dangerous animals, a problem that was to escalate through the boom years of Ireland's tiger economy and leave animals of all sorts displaced and homeless in the subsequent collapse. Cruelty was the only legal grounds with which to seize these animals, and thanks to the legacy of "Humanity Dick" Martin, Ireland had a fine piece of primary legislation called the Protection of Animals Act with which to test and ultimately resolve this stand-off in a court of law. Animal welfare legislation throughout much of the world where law is based on common law, derives from the twin roots of "Humanity Dick" Martin on this side of the Atlantic and Johnny Appleseed on the other.

A team of Gardaí*, wildlife vets brought in from England, welfare professionals and volunteers was assembled. The job of finding sanctuaries for these animals was never going to be easy, but it was done and the next job was to get them out in the Christmas post! Again, all this was done in time. *Sin scéal eile, le leabhar eile!*

Molly presented a problem after being crated. Lifting equipment could not be got down to her quarry residence.

Limerick is renowned for rugby, a ball game chasing an odd-shaped ball that never bounces straight, so the players are ingenious and resourceful. The local rugby teams were called to provide solution and muscle to get Molly and her crate up a steep, narrow incline from the pit. As the work day drew to a close about Limerick and darkness had fallen, big burly men started to arrive at the pit and when enough had assembled they gathered around Molly's crate and in a relentless series of lift and heave movements, they inched Molly to the top. That muscle and will power is why Limerick rugby is famous and a feeder to the national team.

Back at the hotel, which had become our centre of operations, it was the grand dame of animal welfare's pleasure to entertain the rugby players, while my job was to accompany Molly on a truck across Ireland, by ferry across the Irish Sea, and onwards across England to Heathrow airport in time catch a plane to Canada.

Russia did not want the tigers as they had been mongrelised in captivity and could never be returned to the wild or their ancestral home. So they and their cubs were on their way to a wildlife way-station in the United States, and the baboons were sent to Britain.

Canada has long traded and gifted its bears, including polar bears all over the world. Molly was to be the first to make the reverse trip to Canada and this was a powerful message to end the export of wildlife. Molly would arrive to great reception. Separated from her homeland by generations and the Atlantic, deeply institutionalised in Ireland, one had to wonder if anything would be familiar to her.

Though far from hibernating, Molly wished merely to cover herself in straw in her crate, hiding away from all attention. It was best to hibernate or pass through this portal unseen.

In Canada, the spring bear hunt leaves many orphans, so a group of Canadian buddies founded a sanctuary for these with money they'd otherwise have spent on Friday nights. They had a simple and highly effective approach, relocating rogue bears also and generally giving bears good press and a bit of space. Bear With Us,* as they were known and when they heard of Molly, they were eager to offer her a home of enclosed woodland extending out into a lake and the company of another rescued bear. They were passionate about their bears.

As myself and the truck driver whiled away the journey in conversation, many thoughts came to us about the purpose of our mission, all the efforts of all involved to give this little lady bear some dignity and space. We thought it a step toward respect and understanding for an animal that started out much like us, and now, advanced as we are, we wondered at the insecurity of such bullies who still wish to subjugate such creatures.

The crossing on the Irish Sea was storm force and nobody, including the truckers, came to breakfast. I breakfasted alone with the chef to the sound of crashing plates in the galley, and after breakfast, he brought me below decks to see how Molly was faring. She had her head with her great paws over it buried in a corner of the cage, and her haunches high in the air, as though driving underground toward a wished-for den. She was seasick and we left her to it, knowing the journey would have an end in a far better place.

After all the relays, we heard she arrived to a civic reception and her new home.

I was lucky enough to visit her a few years later, and watching her ambling in the company of another bear along the lakeshore and pulling at undergrowth was proof to me that resilient and deep inside Molly, throughout her subjugation, incarceration, and solitude, was a wild Canadian bear. She was back in her homeland, maybe never to roam entirely free, but as well provided for as possible.

I did not even need to whistle up "The Blue Danube Waltz" to see, and I'm sure she'd just have ignored it!

Cometh the Hour,
Cometh the Man

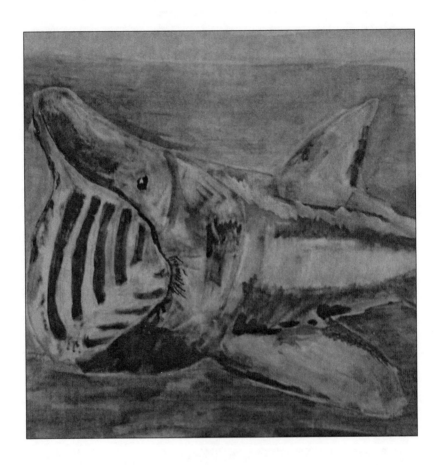

It was a windy day inshore, tops of trees were tossing, and we were pottering around with stock. Two great handlers, sailors, family angels, and friends, the Mermaid Lady and Lucky, were with me.

The house was quiet and children just in from school when a call came through from beach workers of the local authority that a stranded whale about thirteen feet long was found on a nearby beach.

Sad thing, a stranded whale, and often not much you can do

other than witness its demise and sit with it. Some even sing to it.

So we tidied up our tasks and set the stock up for a few hours.

My young ones often liked the journey out, and not expecting to be able to do much for the young leviathan, I brought my son with me on what I expected to be an observer role.

The "angels" were like family to him, so he was quite comfortable with them also.

All of eleven years old, this baby was already talking of becoming a zoologist. His face was beaming with anticipation and excitement and we quietly tried to prepare him for an encounter with less than hopeful outcome. Words were wasted, as I could read his private thoughts and he was going to save the whale!

It was late afternoon in autumn, and Bettystown Beach, County Meath stretched out before us. It was a long sandy beach with a tidal range as wide as the beach was long. It was the ebb of a spring tide and deep water was a long way out. As we approached we could see the white horses breaking a quarter mile out, blown on by the wind with spume over them, the waves losing height and energy, across the long stretch of sand, just as the sad creature they earlier deposited.

An impossible distance without equipment and a skilled team to bring a ton or more of whale back to deep water. We were approaching a small group of workmen, gathered around the whale and my strong son was racing ahead.

It was October and everywhere was grey, land, sea, and sky, and it was as though every force of nature had passed sentence on this poor creature, depositing it at the high water mark to die. The tide had turned, leaving it part buried already, sinking in the wet sand, with more deposited around it by each retreating wave.

Our job could really only be to explain the phenomenon, identify the species, manage expectations, protecting the creature from souvenir hunters or misguided attempts to move it. Ironic how the well-intentioned often cause as much suffering as those of worse intent.

Already its lungs must be collapsing. To move it would be cruelty.

I reached the small circle of men standing in the drizzle. The child and his companions were already there, ahead of me and fully engaged, puzzling over the species and why it had a long, fluting, sabre and upright tail of a shark.

So, change of plan, it was a shark, and no less, a young basking shark at that. Well, not really, it was still thirteen-feet-long, a ton in weight, one-third submerged, two hours recumbent, and almost lifeless.

Explaining the dead and dying to wannabee saviours intent on rescue is always a tough and thankless job, and unbeknownst to yourself, your voice adopts a funereal tone, dropping a few decibels as your posture also slopes. None of the October hat-knocking urges of Ishmael,* signing up to hunt whales for us! We were there to re-float them or sit with them, and a basking shark should be no different. It's hard telling people the best thing to do is do nothing, as often is the case.

As I was trying robotic-like to explain a course of inaction to the solemn and respectful group of workers, my young child, who I would not have brought to a tough rescue for fear of thrashing fluke or violent movements, looked distressed. I looked down at him, his golden curly hair standing out against all the grey, flying in the wind, and tears or drizzle on his pleading face. I did not know which.

As the shark's weakening gills moved ever so slowly, the moments grew longer, with silent protest spreading around the faces. No word was spoken. My authority was disappearing silently to the child among us. It could have been any child, but it was my child.

I did not know what to do and spoke by rote as he broke away from the circle, found a little receptacle among the beach debris, ran to a pool for water, and came running back to the head of the shark, pouring his little offering of life-saving sea water over its great gills, as though anointing it.

We were all silenced as the great still blood suffused gills worked a little harder.

Instantly, his sisters in conspiracy, harbouring no doubt in the child, broke away and resolutely went to his aid, and I could only watch in amazement as the shark responded, even moving its tail a little. Little was significant and less was more, as the mutiny was spreading and I was no longer in command.

The workmen now wanted to help and would only accept positive advice. They were not going to do nothing! They had kept vigil by this great baby shark and doing nothing was no longer an option. One had charge of a big machine with a front-end bucket and had straps. The rest were strapping to work with their shovels. Let no one ever say to me again that council workers only use their shovels to lean on.

My child was now running the show and all I could do was advise and volunteer.

We reached the world's leading basking shark expert on the phone at his workplace in the Isle of Man. He, too, felt it was an impossible case, one never undertaken before. He described the efforts of well-equipped divers freeing tangled basking shark in deep waters and walking them on the ocean bed until they were reoriented.

We were all in new territory and we knew it and still the child was running for water, refilling and bringing it to the shark.

There was to be no going back now, with the light fading and dangers mounting for the walkers taking the shark back into the surf after dark. We had to move fast.

While the child and his guardians continued to work on resuscitation, the machine man brought his great yellow monster of a machine to life and the workers cleared sand furiously with their shovels, so the straps could be passed beneath and around the shark without damaging gills or fins.

Time was now racing and the job was accomplished in minutes. The machine driver started to lift and the machine itself started to tilt, and as it did so, he accelerated towards the surf, the momentum just sufficient enough to suspend the shark in the air and into the sea itself, to the height of his front tyres.

We raced after him fully clothed up to our waists as he dropped his load, apparently undamaged, and reversed out of the water as fast as he had entered.

The rest was up to us!

In the fading light, the shark barely moved his tail, still on his side in the shallow water and side-on to the waves already nudging him shoreward again. We were all in the water, oblivious to the weather, intent on righting this creature and finishing what the child had started. With the nautical expertise of the Mermaid Lady, the handling ability and seamanship of Lucky, and the swell itself, the shark was quickly righted and pointed seawards and the walking started.

The great tail, never violently, started to sweep left to right and right to left with greater strength and frequency.

We were ecstatic and let go. But it was too easy, and he was turned side-on again and rolled. There was to be no mercy here from the sea, and we were now in almost total darkness, with one last opportunity to try the impossible for the shark again, with the workers on the beach wishing and willing us on to success.

We repeated the process and walked the shark longer and farther this time. Darkness was upon us, and we were out farther than we should go safely if the shark rolled or one became pinned under it or lost in the dark, but somehow everyone was unshakeable. We kept voice contact throughout with each other, each now as faith-driven as my son.

In almost total darkness, we simultaneously let go again and watched the shark, while what little night-light left was reflecting off its bulk, propel itself directly forward at right angle through the breaking waves in just about enough depth to keep him buoyant. Thirty feet beyond us, under a break in the cloud cover, we could see his faintly grey and ghostlike outline fade into the night, the tail the last thing to disappear into the darkness.

Back on the beach, it felt like an anti-climax. It had never been done before, that we knew! Had it really happened? Would it turn up beached again the next day?

It was all in a day's work, an attempt at the previously impossible.

Only the child had no doubt. He was cold but impervious, his stringy little bean-stalk frame shivering unconsciously.

It was time for warm clothes and warm food, and the morning would tell its own tale.

The next morning, for miles in either direction, no basking shark re-beached! If it was swimming weakly, the long shore drift would have brought it north. Had it made a half-mile out to sea, and had it remained in the lee of the river wall, it would have come back south. There was no sighting!

There was no media, no photos, and no records of that night, just a few animal handlers and beach workers to account for the impossible and to reassure each other about what was achieved.

The strong son of mine is now a young man and blossoming zoologist, and we only need to remember him to know what was done. To him, it was most natural and remembered simply as the obvious thing to do.

That night on Bettystown* Beach, the child ruled and the shark swam free!

Cometh the hour, cometh the man. My strong son was now a man.

HOBO

Hobo was a truly ugly dog.

No one knew from quite where he came, and he adopted a sentinel position in the new suburbs of the capital city, at a junction on the road leading to Dublin. He was off-black in colour with a porcine stature and disposition, frightening in appearance to all but those that knew him.

Ireland had a horse culture. Dublin had a dog culture in those days. Licensing laws and regulation later brought an end to the era of companion animals in Dublin. In those days, houses and families were known by their dog as much as by surname. Homeless dogs were known by their neighbourhood and there were dogs of all shapes, sizes, and breeds associated with hotels, markets, harbours, and the community that sustained them. There were dogs that sat

66

by graves, empty houses, and pier ends, faithfully awaiting the return of lost owners. There were dogs that ran in packs with young boys and girls, about their street games, feeding house to house from those that would always share a morsel from meagre family sustenance.

Dublin was like Cannery Row* for dogs, and these were known by name and disposition rather than welfare number or licence.

Hobo kept daily point duty at his station, season to season, year after year, sitting patiently and inscrutably on his spot as the inflow of traffic brought workers to the city in the morning and the evening exodus brought them back home for the night.

Ugly and incommunicative though he was, commuters came to know him and miss him if he was not there, because most of the time he was.

Some stopped to feed him from a small distance, often the remains of a packed lunch or doggy bag from canteen or restaurant and he'd accept the morsels after they departed. They'd talk about him during a meal and wonder how he fared. Feeding Hobo became a religious exercise for some.

A small shanty kennel appeared on the earth berm behind his position as well as assorted bits of discarded bedding for his comfort. Pots and pans of after-dinner offerings accumulated around his shanty from the suburban estates behind.

His integration with the community was complete. What affected the community—social problems the great sprawling estates had—Hobo shared!

Hobo was never known to bark or vocalise, and marked all offerings from a slight distance and position of advantage, only indulging after the donor's retreat. His grand isolation was a mark of respect. Years passed in this fashion and he never went hungry or cold.

Rumour had it, on weekends he accompanied one particular family in the neighbourhood to visit a family grave at the cemetery, but this apart, he rarely abandoned his post.

Though he never wore a collar, he was never left short.

The suburbs were fast growing and sprawling, bereft of services, and fast losing connection with the countryside.

One morning the neighbourhood found Hobo homeless again, his kennel burned out, a victim of the growing social problems of rapid urbanisation.

By nightfall, however, a new kennel was put in place, while he observed from a distance. He soon resumed his daily routine as sentinel of that desolate junction, through which everything moved faster and faster, seldom anyone stopping. Hobo bespoke of human kindness and community spirit in the lonely suburban landscape, where displaced humans were transplanted, as much as dogs. As regulation and dog licensing tightened, he evaded the efforts of dog catchers and sustained his lonely vigil over the ever increasing traffic to and from the city. As he aged, his little island shrank and one day he disappeared. His kennel weathered and collapsed into the grassland and eventually the authorities cleaned and sanitised the site.

The family he used to accompany to the cemetery knew nothing of his passing other than the loss, but the story goes he was rescued by animal welfarists and brought to a sanctuary in the countryside to end his days collarless, but with canine companions for the choosing. It was rumoured he lived in canine splendour for a few years more, still collarless and still answering to no name.

The junction among locals is still known as Hobo's Corner.

SWIMMING LESSONS

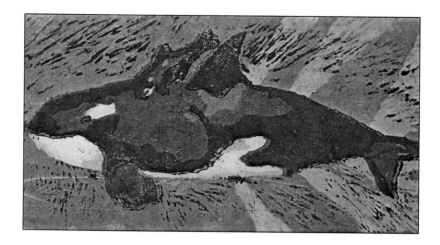

Dublin Bay was our summer playground and a pressure release valve for children in hot weather.

If not for the efforts of a lone campaigner, Dublin Bay Rockall Loftus, many years ago it might have become an oil refinery. The Bay was also outlet for the city's sewage. In those days dilution was viewed as the solution to pollution. Unseen, it was thought to be of no great harm, though the mussels from the Bay could no longer be eaten. Despite the pressures on it with the growth of the city and port, Dubliners claimed it for their own and protections have been increasing over the years, as is the diversity of wildlife returning to it. Not that we, as children, noticed the wildlife too much, other than when exploring rock pools, fishing for crabs, or watching out for jellies, which were the biggest visible threat to swimmers. The invisible threats didn't rate and we didn't notice, so Dubliners from the canals to the Bay were natural swimmers from a young age. Citizens now using the Bay for pleasure and leisure are far more informed and protective about it.

Television was new to Ireland in those years, with limited home produced programmes and hours. When American programmes were imported, we were introduced to a series starring a dolphin called Flipper, suddenly making our Bay look tatty and poor. Little were we to know, till years later, that Flipper, since deceased with many other captive actors, was merely another inhabitant of an illusory TV world. Now wild bottlenose dolphins frequently visit Dublin Bay and it has a resident population of porpoise. Even the whales drop by, and through the encouragement and tuition of whale-watchers, we've learned to look for them. Children bathing in the Bay and around Ireland are conscious of these animals, though unseen, while entering the kingdom of the whale, waters now a whale and dolphin sanctuary. Post-national independence, it has taken at least three generations of Irish children to discover what was always ours to enjoy.

* * *

When I was a young man, a travelling dolphin show came to town, to the very showground, I was working on. It could never happen now, but at that time these were to be the stars of a Christmas show, never before on view in Ireland and the crowds flocked to see them perform in a small, circular, unheated pool under cover from the elements.

I came in early every morning just to spend time observing them and sit with them and one morning I asked the trainer if I could swim with them. To my surprise she agreed, and the next morning and for many after, I was in the cold water with the dolphins before the day's work began. The energy in the pool could have lit and powered the city. I was but flotsam in the water as they swam by, under, over, and around me. I suppose I was some temporary distraction in their confinement and certainly they appeared to welcome me and even indulge me occasionally, just hanging suspended, eye-balling, sonar full on and touching gently. I came earlier and earlier and stayed in the water as long as I could endure the temperature. When I would sit on the side and begin to leave, they'd stay by me, one or the other sometimes resting its beak between my knees.

I was living for these moments, and the job was secondary. As our games developed and I spent more time beneath the surface, I was to hear underwater what at the time I thought the most beautiful music and whistles I had ever heard. Soon after they were gone, and it was only years later I learned these were cries and signals of distress. How long they lived after and how they died, I do not know.

They had cried out to me and I failed to respond, instead revelling in their confinement and distress, unbeknownst to myself.

In the years that followed, I was to meet wild bottlenose dolphins around the coast of Ireland, and my life partner and young family were to enjoy far more positive experiences with these free-living creatures in the wild that need the full and broad expanses of sea around the little rock of Ireland.

* * *

Dingle was a tiny town nestled under the mountains on a rocky peninsula, the most westerly part of Ireland, and nearest point to America. Everything the capital was, Dingle was the reverse. Dublin was large, smoggy, dirty, noisy, and crowded. Dingle was small, pristine, clean, and sparse, swept by the winds and waves of the Atlantic. For Dubliners discovering it along the Atlantic seaboard, it was a leap to freedom beyond imagination. Eagles once soared here and were being brought back. What a place for any wild creature! You could feel yourself turning feral here.

Word was spreading of a friendly wild dolphin, a rare phenomenon, taking up residence at the mouth of Dingle Bay.

Dingle had a strong claim on me. A government office had banished me to work there one winter, a punishment I thoroughly enjoyed. I fell in love with Dingle, and discovered love there during my exile. I would avail of any excuse to go back west,* and what better reason than to meet this friendly dolphin. And meet him I did, many times.

I was just a plain swimmer, without snorkel, flippers, suit, board, kayak, or other accessories giving speed and manoeuvrability in the water, and to which the dolphin was hugely attracted. My plan was to go down to meet him early in the mornings, before others were about. Entering the water the first morning, with a couple of stones to bang together beneath the surface, I was almost immediately in the company of the dolphin. On banging the stones, I could see a dorsal fin cutting the water, rising and falling beneath, in a direct line toward me, and there he was, huge in the shallows, beak between my knees.

Mornings of pleasure and exhilaration followed, as he stretched me more and more, and he'd consort with everyone entering his domain throughout the rest of the day. Often we'd watch from the shore and even visited him one evening by boat at his place of sleep, in the company of the first diver he befriended and who was minder to him, thereafter.

I believe my son was conceived about that time.

We returned with our children, and as they grew strong in the water, they were to meet another very wild female dolphin in County Clare.* She, too, had her favourite spots and drew swimmers from far and wide who sought the ultimate dolphin experience.

Bottlenose dolphins are big, powerful, wild creatures, capable of inflicting mortal injury with a single blow, and this dolphin had hospitalised a few overly-familiar swimmers in salutary warning to all.

Going to meet her, we adopted the same plan as used at Dingle and quietly entered her waters in the quiet times, gently rattling a few pebbles in a bottle beneath the surface. My children were rewarded with days of swimming in a most glorious little bay, with a wild free-living dolphin on its own terms. Already strong swimmers, the dolphin stretched the two children and they followed. They remain two gloriously confident swimmers to this day, as at ease in the dolphin's watery realm as their own.

Unlike my own earlier experiences, theirs was on equal, respectful, and independent terms, and the great tribute the wild dolphin was to pay their respect, was to remain around to play together.

I was witnessing cross-species communication and remained an outsider to this communication between innocents. I have an enduring image of my children tired and resting across seaweed-covered rocks in that bay at low tide, and the dolphin beak beached, just waiting for them to recover and start play again.

Since then another friendly dolphin has appeared around Torai Island, the most north westerly point of Ireland, befriending a local dog. Resident pods are being identified around the island, and others have delighted walkers, bathers, and water users around Dublin Bay itself, by their visits in recent years.

Sadly the "Flipper industry" of captive dolphins has grown exponentially, confining thousands of them worldwide in cruel conditions, where they are condemned to short, miserable, and lonely lives. Flipper's trainer* devoted his life and career, after the series ended, to campaigning for dolphin freedom and an end to the cruelty.

People from all over the world now come to Ireland for the ultimate dolphin experiences, just to see them on their own terms, in their realm.

They're *out there*, but don't tell the orderlies!

From my Father's Chair

A first generation granny of the suburbs, framed by a window, looks out on a verdant suburban garden and the constant and changing traffic passing through it.

Many of the creatures passing her view have their routines while others continually surprise.

In still thought, her memories can transport her back to the first habitations of the newly emerging estate and its first inhabitants.

As the builders moved ahead, eating up fertile land spreading across the foothills of the Dublin Mountains, leaving rows of houses on barren plots in their wake, the new settlers took to the task of creating gardens and healing the land. They were a mix of city and country folk in the new estates, diverse in background and culture, inventive, and with a range of skills among them.

This cultural melting pot was to be a great, unplanned, social experiment, and the results and diversity were inevitably to be reflected in the gardens and green spaces as they toiled to heal the land and the close relations with the wild neighbours that would evolve. These wild co-habitants paid no rent or mortgage, but would nevertheless become part of many household budgets.

In the first instance, there were just the sparrows as any evidence of life before the settlement or providing any continuity with earlier inhabitants. These and views of the distant mountains, of seabirds wheeling overhead under disturbed and changing cloudscape and angry skies, were the only reminders of a greater nature beyond the houses. Settlers brought dogs, cats, hens, racing pigeons, and other assorted domestics, all reliant and attached to households, but initially the estates were fortresses and wild nature was locked out.

Over the years, as the soil improved and hedges and trees grew and thickened, insects and birds returned. Robins were followed by their big cousins, blackbirds and thrushes. The little wren found nesting sites. Finches of all sorts, more colourful relations of the sparrow, came in waves. Starlings, another great urban dweller, visited in large flocks. Even hawks returned to fly the hedge lines, diving after prey who sheltered in trees and hedge. Young hawks sometimes crashed into spotless windows allowing light clear through the houses back to front, so house proud were the residents of their new homes.

As the gardens established and residents became more comfortable, many unwittingly turned to labour-saving industrial products. Gardens were to be sanitised with molluscicides, aphicides, insecticides, herbicides, biocides, and other killing -icides, proclaiming to take the drudgery and toil out of gardening, boost production, and replace old fashioned husbandry and rotation.

Bird populations again waned, many species disappearing like the sparrow. *Silent Spring** had come to the gardens now of plenty, but a music and verve was missing and gardeners began to feel a lonesomeness of spirit about their beloved plots, not unlike the feeling of Native Americans at the passing of the great herds of bison. Something was wrong in Eden.

Cats, domestic and feral, descendants of Egyptian ancestors were, with every settlement and more recent introduced Asian magpies spreading across the land were highly successful colonisers, exploiting their closeness to human habitations and exercising their advantage against the native birds. Pressure had reached critical mass and, for a while, wild native birds and small mammals were to be the losers.

However, many of the first grandparents of the first estates were retiring from active gardening, looking to the garden as a place of pleasure and leisure to be shared with grandchildren, and delighting in occasional sightings of wildlife. Where they toiled to rear families was again becoming commons with the wildlife, sharing space and corridors to the greater wild beyond the estates.

Many of the greying gardeners were abandoning chemicals and allowing much of their holdings to revert to nature. A transformation was again taking place, and the birds came back in all their glorious colour and variety. That is all, on quiet reflection, but the dowdy dunnocks, house and hedge sparrows, and their quiet memory and mystery outstanding brought a smile to the face of an old woman who'd seen it from the start. The sparsity of sparrows in the suburbs remains unsolved. Had the suburbs become too gentrified for these early companions?

Bird food became a weekly item on grocery lists, and all sorts of accessories from bird tables to baths to nest boxes and ponds were provided. It became *de rigeur* to provide for the birds. Wildlife is held in great affection in the modern suburbs.

* * *

When the weekly toil is done, hard-working modern suburbanites often like to congregate in places of pleasure, relax in conversation, and revel in storytelling. One such place could be reached by Magic Carpet and a famous incident took place there, one late summer's evening, illustrating the high standing of wildlife in the suburbs.

A happy company was gathered around a table when a black cat strolled in from the darkness, largely unnoticed and carrying a bird in its mouth. The reaction of two kindly women noticing this was explosive, and taking the entire company by surprise, they dived simultaneously on the cat to release its tiny prey. The cat left very surprised and the company was left with a solitary sparrow, not yet fledged and still alive. Tail and wing feathers only just emerging, it could do no more than wobble on its little legs and present a wide yellow gape.

The shooting of an American bald headed eagle, the national bird of the US, would not have sparked such response as an attack on a sparrow in the suburbs of Dublin, so iconic is its standing.

A little bowl lined with tissue was quickly found to substitute for a nest and sanctuary. My hopes were not high that this downy chick could survive the gape of a feline as few ever did, but the rescuers believed otherwise, and so it was to become my constant companion and desk accessory for the next fortnight.

It gaped constantly till satisfied with morsels of grated hardboiled egg and wholemeal bread and drinks from an eyedropper and then a powernap, head under its wing for minutes, until hunger stirred it again.

After that short growth spurt, it was hopping around the desk picking at morsels, punctuating paperwork, and testing its wings, till the day came to take its leave into a leafy hedgerow connecting an arable field in search of a flying flock of its own kind and freedom again.

The rescuers were far-seeing, utterly vindicated, and testimony to the affection in which wildlife is held in Dublin and its suburbs. Birds that neither sow nor reap but simply cheer and delight are held in high esteem.

In many countries now, city and suburban gardens provide as much wildlife habitat as national parks, and the principle revenue of many garden centres has become wild food and accessories.

* * *

Sitting in my father's chair, looking out his widow's window on a garden of memories that both he and my mother lovingly restored after the builders, where children played and a family was reared, a fresh page and new life is turned to present my mother with daily theatre. As the garden matures and returns to wildlife, she and many like her are presented with a window on nature bustling with activity, to their entertainment and enjoyment, separated by only a pane of glass so habituated and welcomed the creatures have become to the early settlers and ageing residents.

As I leave, dozens of blackbirds are feeding on the apples fallen from an ageing apple tree, planted in the garden's first year. A thrush is bathing in a birdbath, scattering translucent droplets which appear like a pulsating aura about him. There is a rainbow-coloured frenzy of finches on the feeders, and starlings rotate with them, sweeping in and out in swathes. The old man saw all this before the arrival of the suburbs, and the old lady, those neighbours remaining and their successors now have gallery boxes on star-studded dramas unfolding daily, rivalling the great theatres of the city. They tell me now of their herons and foxes and squirrels visiting openly by day, and hedgehogs and other creatures of the night setting off night sensors and security lights.

For lifetime's toil and stewardship, shouldn't every ageing person, as of right, have access to such pleasant outlooks over land or sea and access to nature? Would this and variations of this not be the true meaning of pleasing environment for a dignified old age?

National health systems worldwide, please take note.

Maybe and Maybe Not

Ever think you had a role to play in wildlife welfare, conservation or the protection of endangered species? Feed the birds over winter? Bring a wildlife road casualty to the vet?

Can ordinary, urbanised or rural folk know what to do when confronted with wildlife orphans or casualties? So far are they removed from us and our conventional, mainstream approach to health and recovery, even the scientist and vet are often confounded!

We mostly accept life, casualty, and death without intervention, as a given when confronted with wild creatures, and seldom pause to think of the exacerbated threats they face, arising from our colonisation of wild spaces. Do they not, too, require second chances, brief sanctuary, and respite to recover and survive?

It was the Christmas holiday when two scallywag cubs were sent to us from a veterinary surgery on the Corrib River in Galway, in the west of Ireland, for recovery. Immediate aid and veterinary intervention had been provided and the cubs arrived roisterous, boisterous, and intent on defence and aggressive, though barely weaned off milk and still dependent. Seemed a doddle, till we tried to handle them, when it became apparent in defence they were likely to self-destruct. Their high-tensioned, spring-like skeletons could coil like a snake, turn themselves inside-out, rotating and leveraging off their cranial axis. Handling was more like an exorcism.

Siblings we knew them to be, rescued after their mother had been killed by a dog, but of indeterminate sex arising from inability to examine, and so it would remain until other clues were provided. So they were simply christened "Maybe" and "Maybe Not," maybe girl, maybe a boy. One merely needed feeding, the other regular flushing through a cranial wound inflicted by the dog. The wound was enough to distinguish one from the other until we got to know them better. It was the clue to separating them, as so fast were they about your feet, the one would blend into the other and unfailingly reverse positions! It was like a three-card trick, and the only way of being sure which was which, was to bin one while examining the other.

Intent on survival without human intervention, their uninterpretable protestations exceeded "click" language, varying across menacing *miaows* to squeaks to staccato chatter. Truly wild, they objected to all aid and intervention, were more agile than cats, spinally and curvaceously defying all restraints. It took all the efforts of two hominids to daily restrain one to simply flush its wound, the other protesting still from inside a bin, and to finally establish they were brother and sister otter cubs.

Thankfully, though the cure appeared worse than the condition, we prevailed to cleanse the double aperture head wound and we were elated when it healed and closed. Appetites were undiminished despite forceful interventions and they ate fastidiously on fish and occasional fowl. Our fingers miraculously intact, despite bite marks on every piece of equipment, we were able to retreat from their cage, other than to present food and water, and consider long term release.

Maybe and Maybe Not, two young otter cubs born out of season, their mother lost to a hound and parachuted in on us for Christmas, were now eating their way out of confinement. Even metal was only a temporary obstacle! The holiday had to be spent erecting an enclosure, kennel, and pool for their convalescence and weaning back to the wild.

Anecdotally, historically there had been otters in this area criss-crossed and traversed by deep ditches, connecting with distant water courses, and so likely suitable as anywhere for the long slow release required for young otters, so long is their learning curve for independence off the mother.

Exceptionally clever and opportunistic animals, from the moment of their introduction to their new home, they immediately set about redesigning the kennel, changing the bedding arrange-ments, and dismantling straw bales to build a perfect holt* of straw with u-tube entrances facing south, easily defended. Our sole pur-pose became the provision of food for as long as the enclosure could contain them, as the release would be inevitable and at their discre-tion. Within a couple of months, they engineered their escape, though returned nightly for food.

This was rehabilitation according to otter rules, and as long as we did not interfere, they made full use of this soft release to point they'd happily feed within feet of us. The rule was no touching, so we enjoyed their nocturnal antics and chattering for months to come with ever longer intervals away, as they ranged farther, feeding from wild sources also.

A great dog otter appeared one day, no doubt in search of the female, and was led to our home by the network of river, streams, and ditches, and this suggested their release and dispersion seemed complete. They had crossed paths with their elusive wild relations.

Shockingly, the young dog of the siblings was found dead on a road after about a year free, and the female was never seen again. The adage speed kills applies to wildlife also, and roads that connect us and our habitations, divide wildlife.

We like to think the sister survived and the appearance of another wild otter augurs well for otter in the neighbourhood.

Maybe and Maybe Not remain evidence of this rare and elusive creature's ability to survive in our changed landscape, if we are but aware of them. Hidden and unseen, need not mean gone.

Femoral Knob
Ostectomy

One of the most accommodating and compliant wild animals I have ever had to care for was Bernie, as she came to be known for her time in care, a little elderly badger sow.

She had been hit by the post-van on a little used back road in the area, during the Christmas post rush and the postman, distraught, had contacted the local vets, who in turn referred her to our small sanctuary.

Cold, immobile, and unconscious by the roadside, laying in the wet, she looked a poor bedraggled specimen indeed and more like roadkill, but the postman knew her to be still alive.

Carefully, as we had all heard of the bite of the badger and stories of their ferocity and courage to the end when defending their cubs and setts or barbarically pitted against dogs, we lifted her onto a blanket and into a cage and a car. We did not want her to wake till adequately caged, and caution was to be our guide in all further dealings.

With sleep patterns the reverse of our own, we rarely catch sight of live badgers, other than occasionally in car headlights at night. Living below the tree line in ancient underground setts, in a tight-knit community, moving little in winter, they remain elusive and mysterious. Familiar to most of us by story and the death-mask like appearance of their all too common corpses on roads, our knowledge is as much anecdotal as scientific.

Wild animals crossing our fields of activity often suffer unimaginable consequences, perish, and disappear quietly. Roadways, fencing, overhead lines, shipping, and flight paths, high-rise buildings, night illuminations, and multiple other human invention and activity, are cutting across traditional and ancient territories and movements across the earth, learned, inherited, and hardwired over generations for many species. As the earth is zoned, cut, and compartmentalised into management units, entire species in our time are disappearing forever, at a pace faster than the last great mass extinctions. Token attempts are made to manage some of the more iconic, critical, and visible casualties, who are no longer fully wild, in ever smaller territories or captivity.

Badgers allegedly have been a reservoir and at the frontline of bovine tuberculosis transmission in many countries and a threat to Ireland's island and agrarian economy, which is hugely dependent on the cattle industry. In the eyes of many, this added to their infamy. So zealous were many in this belief that the young State sponsored their persecution at huge cost, described in the last century by a governor of the Central Bank as the "greatest financial scandal in the history of the state." This century, thus far, has revealed ever greater financial scandals, human offenders, and practises of scapegoating. Science has since vindicated the badger somewhat, and history and people have begun to look more kindly on this most shy of animals.

* * *

Despite all this history and baggage, the postman, residents, and local vets in this traditional farming community wanted to give this badger a chance.

She was underweight, noted as elderly by her worn teeth, with bite marks about her haunches and abroad at Christmas in daylight and inclement weather. All this was mysterious, and it was surmised that she may have been driven from her set for some unknown reason. Later she was to test clear on disease. More often than not, we have to recognise there are more questions than answers, but it was clearly in our gift* to provide some help and a possible second chance to this badger, and the consensus was clear. Good will for badgers abounded that Christmas.

For wildlife casualties, very often sanctuary is just the space and time to heal and it is important not to engage in a tyranny of nursing, compromising the animal's long-term rehabilitation and release prospects. It is a fine balance endlessly improving between vets, scientists, rehabilitators and rescuers, species by species and individual by individual.

Bernie had a lifetime's experience, and despite her immediate life-threatening condition, was to be largely her own physician, excepting one extraordinary intervention by one extraordinary vet.

Still dazed and under severe restraint, she was recovering in warmth as fluids were administered and her bite wounds cleaned and dressed. For the duration no one quite relaxed, when restraining her though, she never struggled or cried out, so powerful is the suggestion and reputation of the bite of even a sick or dying badger. Small though she was, she was a mass of dense muscle, powered from the rear for tunnelling and burrowing. Food was at ground level, refuge was below, and she seemed mostly pointed in a downward direction, rarely raising her head skywards except when relaxed and unobserved. Poorly sighted, her other senses were acute and she was ever alert as she recovered and started controlling her own environment. Holding position was her only protest to handling, to the point that we learned to work around her.

There was no outward evidence of injury as a result of the collision with the post-van, but one hind quarter did seem somewhat disabled as she tried to move more. So with the aid of a small field X-ray machine, anaesthesia, and a lifetime's experience and improvisation, a wonderful vet declared the problem as a displaced hip that was an old injury which was reignited by the accident. Bernie had survived not just the collision but an older injury as well, and must have been in ongoing pain. True to form, this vet also had a solution. She proposed an operation, common even in humans in the days before modern hip replacements. She wished to perform a femoral knob ostectomy. I can only attempt to repeat her explanation in simple terms. This involved open surgery on the ball-and-socket joint of the hip, shaving off the displaced ball, and thus relieving rubbing, pain, and inflammation. In the absence of a working joint, the bones could fuse to give either a rigid leg or the musculature compensates to provide a rubbery one. Either way it worked for many humans in the past and the badger would be left with a functioning, if slightly impaired hind quarter. It couldn't be simpler to a vet, so we put faith in our vet and Bernie's fate in her care, and all worked as it was meant to work.

Bernie became immediately more mobile, and as the wound closed and reduced to a scar across the large shaved area of the operation site, she was moved to a shed and open enclosure, to start fending for herself. Straw and hay was thrown in for bedding, and as she got stronger she could dig her way out. Her own physician, she would also engineer her own release!

* * *

To our surprise, Bernie did not venture out as early as anticipated.

She made a sett of the straw and hay, disappearing under it entirely, but leaving two distinct entrances. As she went deeper, the domed roof went higher and more bedding was added. When food was provided, her mask would appear at one entrance, but she would not emerge until alone. Amazingly, she seemed all too comfortable and forgotten was the "call of the wild" or even others of her own kind.

In early March, we heard weak squeaking from deep within her straw and hay sett. Alarmed, initially we thought rats had moved in to squat, as they already raided the food bowl and might pose some danger to her, but she remained unalarmed and continued to appear eagerly for her food, awaiting our departure to fully emerge. As the days progressed, the squeaking became stronger and more urgent, Bernie's appetite was great, "the penny dropped,"* and someone declared Bernie to have given birth to cubs! The "lights switched on," and in an instant of simultaneous recall everyone remembered the phenomenon of delayed implantation* in badgers! What instinct or intelligence possessed her to remain safe and make the best of an alien environment for what stirred within her and to nurse and rear them, till they were strong enough to follow her back to the wild? The sett was now a nest and we were afraid to inspect or disturb too early for fear of disturbing the nursing mother.

Bernie had settled into her routine and after about a month, we carefully peeled away the roof of the sett. Bernie emerged and waited calmly and guardedly in a corner of the shed while I reached down a tunnel to a warm chamber below, still wondering would I find rats or badger cubs and would the latter bite? I found a solitary, well developed, wriggling, protesting, badger cub, already the look-alike of its calm mother. Confirming it a little lone male, I returned it immediately, replacing the roof of the sett. Bernie returned swiftly to the urgent calls below and so they were left to their own devices from there.

Was it the result of anaesthesia that there was but one cub?

Was it the result of delayed implantation? This one cub survived collision, trauma, anaesthesia and, operation. What a mother!

We were lucky to be able to observe them at feed and play thereafter by closed circuit TV provided by a volunteer, and they provided endless hours of entertaining viewing for volunteers on night shifts.

At the end of June, Bernie dug in beneath her shed with her cub, now half her size. She was now free to roam at will and explore her surroundings beyond the sett that stood her so well. After a few days, she returned no more and the rats had the food bowl to themselves.

Toward the end of that summer, an early morning driver spotted a badger mother with well grown cub in tow, crossing a road nearby. She was travelling well and instantly recognisable by a bald flank at the site of the femoral knob ostectomy, where the hair had still not fully regrown.

Other badgers reside in this area. Without a sett would this twosome be the last of their line? Where would they reside for the winter? Would they integrate or be welcomed into another sett? Would Bernie set up a solitary, lone-parent sett, as she already proved capable? Would she give birth again? How long would her solitary cub stay with her? Would he be the founder of a new line?

Badgers remain mysterious, and Bernie was one mysterious old badger sow.

MIDNIGHT AT X-ROADS

We picked a small remote corner of Ireland to rear a family. Forgotten beyond Dublin was Fingal, the thirty third county of Ireland, reputedly the most hedge-rowed part of the country, hiding many private *bothies*,* cabins, *clocháns*, and houses.

Fingal* or Fionn Ghall, the Land of the Fair-haired Stranger, was reputedly the first landfall of the Vikings and had many waves of invasion and colonisation, before and since. More Round and Martello towers* than any other part of the country testify to the wave-on-wave of races that crossed this ancient county.

Here Gall lived alongside Gael, even to descendants of Cromwell's, O'Brien's, Donnelly's and more, to this day.

The small fields, where they remain, conceal many habitats and species. Ours was the field of the frogs, a generous Irish acre, home since I don't know when to masses of frogs and newts.

The quiet rural children of the area encounter many species from their own natives to the travelling or passing aliens. Bison graze the fields alongside Herefords and more popular cattle.

Much like the field of dreams, when Muhammad would not go to the mountain, it had to come to him, so flights of fancy and imagination resulted in many species over time ultimately visiting and settling in Fingal, as well as many races of people. Tobergregan, Garristown was a cosmopolitan place. There were creatures of day and night and twilight and worlds between with room for all.

Hedgehogs came with the Normans for food and when a giant hedgehog was reported, nobody dismissed it or was too surprised.

After midnight one night, a neighbouring gentleman and his daughter appeared at our window to proclaim presence of a porcupine on a back road, coming from the local town. He had recently been surprised by the presence of a porcupine on a holiday in northern Italy, and certainly knew his porcupines from his onions. He even claimed to have a picture of this beast, running alongside it on the road before it took to the fields. He showed me the picture, but all I could see was black on black and puzzled how difficult it must be to get a picture of an African porcupine, more black than white, on a dark unlit road at midnight with a camera without a flash. It's a bit like searching for a black cat in a windowless dark room.

This man was not given to flights of fancy and was backed up fully by his young daughter. Funnily too, in the recesses of her mind, my sleepy spouse recalled news of a new zoo park opening some few miles across the fields. An interesting interruption to the evening, but we all went to bed imagining the dark creature lost to the night.

During the next month there were sightings over a large area, some after public house hours, and rumours abounded about the large hedgehog-like creature. The local zoo boss had meanwhile confirmed a missing "porky pine," noting that it might lack bulk to eat but could forage indefinitely in the Irish countryside. He advised it could be lured into a shed with food of vegetarian variety and was particularly attracted to potatoes, cooked or uncooked. The rumour machine went into overdrive and the hunt was up.

Many a lion had died in Africa of infected muzzle and mouthful of porcupine quills, and dogs were to be discouraged.

Funny how rescue calls and these creatures generally present themselves at midnight, but about a month later another neighbour from Nutstown-X, a nearby crossroads, called late to ask me down, as our spiny-quilled escapee had appeared at the back of her home and was heading for a small orchard, with her husband and son in pursuit, trying to keep it in sight.

The lady of the X-roads who made the call was a great animal lover and among her many gifts was that of feeding young swallows and house martens, difficult for even the most experienced bird handlers. It was said she could catch flies out of the air, between her fingers, to feed her lost chicks when needed.

Her success was legendary, and like all good animal handlers, she called in all help available when presented with a new problem.

A yard brush with long stiff bristles is a wonderful tool for a porcupine capture, coupled with a stout box and herding boards. The upturned brush sliding low to the ground underneath the porky's rear and batteries of quills makes him feel vulnerable and exposed and drives him forward. This is time-tested technique tried on many animals and a variation on the theme of "grabbing the balls and mind and heart will follow." The porcupine likely thinks the bristles another porcupine of no good intent by such approach, and, short-sighted and facing forward in the dark, who's he to argue till at least he has view of his assailant?

The lady of the X-roads was at her gate, standing by her children, when I arrived and directed me down the road, where a posse had followed the elusive beast. These included neighbours, help from the local pub, and two passing armed detectives in all. X-roads are excellent gathering points for rallies and posses.

We were poorly equipped with feeble torches, but the hunt was up and none of these men were going home without an effort.

The sabred quarry had gone into a small orchard with lots of cover, so we skirted the boundaries to drive him toward the centre and not let him break through a boundary hedge, as cleverly he had already calculated his best escape route. Time and again we found him but failed to drive him toward the box. Each time he was encountered, quills would rattle and he'd go into attack mode in reverse, as is customary for "porky pines," and scatter the defenceless and confused herders. "Savaged by a dead sheep" was the mood summed up by one of the posse after another failed attempt. The herders, however, were not to be daunted, instead growing in unison and determination.

The only hope was to get him to a small open space unobstructed by trees. The porcupine understood the strategy also and many times he repelled in reverse, dropped his quills, concealing the white and scurried back into darkness beyond the torch beams.

On one occasion an overly ambitious and frustrated herder armed with a dust bin he'd found and catching brief sight of his quarry, came crashing through an apple tree, launching himself from a height in desperation more than intent, slamming down his bin, only to miss!

The porcupine flew off like a buzz saw blade, loose of its fastenings, quills rattling like staccato fire. Everyone scattered in the dark, not knowing from what direction the reversing, rapid-firing creature was coming from, other than by sound of its quills. Now everyone knew the potential of our little quarry, no heavier than a collie dog but ready to drive quills in reverse through to ankle and shin bones. He routed nine men and temporarily escaped. We were humbled and crestfallen. The next attempt had to be better planned and regimented. If ever a group of defeated men was galvanised for a last determined effort, this was it.

Retreating again back to the hedgerows, his departure from the field was prevented and apple tree by apple tree, row by row, he was shepherded invisibly but centrally again, and the slow drive forward to the open space began. We had learned a lesson and maintained a steady line. So, too, had the porcupine. Having routed us before, every now and then, he reversed suddenly, quills quivering to break the line closing behind him.

We were steadier and more patient, and by bluff and counter

bluff the little creature was finally central to a circle of nine men—
more than a match you might think—but he was not going to be
caught without some resistance.

Short-sightedly the "porky pine" sized up his adversaries by their
feet. He probably could not even see their faces in the dark. Every
so often he'd stamp a foot, grunt, set quills rattling, hips swinging,
and waltz a little in reverse, then ricochet off his central position
like a Ouija suddenly energised by an evil spirit.

By maintaining the line and a couple of encounters with the
mysterious other porcupine or yard bush he reversed into, there
ensued a quiet and calm stand-off.

Without herding boards, there would be one opportunity to
jump him with the box or lose him again. The box handlers moved
quietly and patiently, without throwing shadows and were successful! Underneath the box quills rattled on the sides in crescendo,
signalling the end to a drumming performance. Nine men danced
and joked like children, clearly fulfilled and vindicated, and equally
relieved.

A few apples and bananas in the box kept the captive happy
overnight, till reunited with his mate next day, whom he promptly
spiked to make room at the feeding dish.

The detectives announced no casualties and none missing in
action, as everyone wended off home wondering was there really,
finally closure.

Many races and many species continue to wash over Fingal and
places like it, and lives are never as quiet and uneventful as the
rumoured rural idyll. Rural people are always prepared. That was
the night of the "Tobergregan porky pine," or African crested porcupine as he was variously known, ending a month-long break for
freedom and becoming for a while an addition to local fauna. Red
kites and grey partridge are being reintroduced, but where is the
raven, red deer, and bear?

When the evidence of our lives is disassembled molecule by

molecule and atom by atom, does it not return reassembled in some form or even reunited in time? Are we not weaved and woven with the lives and bodies of other creatures and wholly united in one entity?

When a porcupine from Africa appears among the fields and hedgerows of Ireland, do we not pause to ask great questions? Can the monkey with a typewriter, in time, create a Shakespearean sonnet? Can the beat of a butterfly's wings ultimately raise a storm? Unwitnessed, does the tree in the forest fall silently?

What was a porcupine really doing in Tobergregan?

THE NATIVE AMERICAN
AND THE IRISH STOAT

Travelling to the village for supplies one day on a back country road, I saw a small brown pelt creamed like butter to the tarmac ahead of me. A feral mink! I slowed down, giving it berth to see the distinct black tail-tip of the native stoat, and as I passed, respecting the dead road casualty, I saw a little pink mouth gape and head raised, no bigger than a blackberry.

Stopping the jeep immediately, I got out, as I thought to witness its last gape and breath, and incredibly, even with tyre treads evident across the wee would-be corpse, it was still alive.

Intuitively following the rehabilitators' creed to assist wildlife and life, I literally scraped it from the tarmac and took it home, back to the sanctuary, with no notion of further prospects.

The Irish stoat is renowned in folklore for its funerals, assemblies, and marches, but rarely seen beyond stone wall country. Historically, much of this area was stone wall country, well grown over by hedgerows and years of cultivation, with stoats anecdotally reported.

We followed protocol, intubating the limp body with still beating heart, all that seemed alive of the creature. The body had started to swell like a marrowfat pea. Repeating this procedure, we still had a living juvenile stoat on our hands, now standing on tiny legs and raising itself up to every approach, inflated as a balloon.

The tiny skeleton seemed unbroken, regardless of the great

vehicle that pancaked it.

The famed and ferocious hunter, capable of killing a rabbit many times its size as well as birds landing close to its hedgerow hide, was alive and feeding. This was now like a resurrection, so we introduced small pieces of chicken, which it set upon. Still in a cage, I gave this little hunter some diced chicken on its third day, which it attacked with rapidity, suddenly doing a backwards somersault, and then it flopped again, corpse-like to the back of its cage.

Once again confronted with expiry, I shouted for the assistance of an excellent Native American animal handler, with the sanctuary at that time, for spectacles and forceps. She had nothing to hand but a scissors, and as precious seconds ticked away we held the lifeless creature, mouth prised open, to remove the piece of chicken obstructing the passage of life-giving air and oxygen.

Time was not our friend, so short-sightedly, gambling, not knowing whether it was the offending piece of chicken or the stoat's tongue, we luckily extracted the meat.

The creature was still lifeless over my colleague's hand and she immediately put mouth-to-mouth and blew. She then put the full head of the stoat into her mouth and blew again until the tiny body kicked again back to life. Yet another resurrection!

I was lost in admiration for my Native American colleague, who so often before quietly seemed to know just what to do, protocols, procedures, and medical discipline apart!

All this happened in minutes and again we had a live, vibrant, hunting stoat on our hands, interested in nothing but food, which we diced smaller or left him to tear apart as he grew stronger.

Two resurrections later and we were still bragging about the stoat, who sadly put his head through the mesh of his cage to meet his maker by the jaws of a feral cat.

Cats do not belong in sanctuaries. Like the frog and scorpion crossing the river, they follow their nature and the lion is not yet ready to lay down with the lamb.

We saw it again with a lonesome last seal of the season, presenting fish to a visiting heron. After days of offerings, the heron removed one eye, setting the seal's rehabilitation after surgery back by a month. Thankfully the one-eyed seal survived and prospered to release, but the rules of nature are unbending and survival lessons need to be well-learned.

Many escapees and domestics wander Ireland to the detriment and destruction of otter and fowl, and natives such as the stoat must struggle to survive the competition of aliens. We still like to believe stoats survive in this area, on the evidence of unfortunate road kills, in refuges of deeply buried stone walls, beneath the hedgerow-clad field boundaries of Fingal. The intuitive knowledge and actions of the visiting Native American also testify to the fact that we can still address the odds.

Aren't the black-footed ferrets, once the world's rarest terrestrial mammal, still alive on the North American plains, thanks to their own resilience and the efforts of conservators and wildlife rehabilitators?

When an animal or species is on the brink, it is the wildlife rehabilitators who lend successful conservation its cutting edge.

ROAD TO WORLD WHALE SANCTUARY

Among whale folk the outward search for sanctuary ultimately and inevitably has as its zenith a world whale sanctuary. By measured steps from childhood, through the stages of man, rebirths, successive civilisations, and wherever you're coming from yourself, we reach closer and closer, never quite getting there. And when our labour has exhausted us and enlightenment eluded us, in rest we realise sanctuary resides within, however we toil without. Sanctuary is a word that has defied definition. It is as much about the quest as the conquest and the journey as the destination. And so the search for sanctuary is a carousel, we step on and off, putting shoulder to wheel and appointed tasks, where effort and comradeship are the reward, rather than the result. Sanctuary is of the heart and the more true hearts bond together, the greater its embrace on our external world.

So it is worthwhile to relate one such sanctuary story I was privileged to witness and be part of, a story not yet ended, which may be the greatest of all in search for sanctuary, and that is the tale of the Irish Whale and Dolphin Group who gave life to the sanctuary of the same name.

Following a drizzly November of the soul and the exhortations of one Gabriel of the quayside, a simple summons was sent out across the island of Ireland that was to bring together a quiet, shuffling group of men and women on December 1, 1990, to meet in a toxic building in the capital City. As apprehensive and hypo as Ishmael amidst whale-hunting men that first night in the Spouters' Inn, this group set to chart a new future for the whale. As sure as St. Elmo's fire charged the lances and chilled the souls of Ahab's harpooners in their monomaniacal quest for the great white whale, a spark ignited among that group, uniting them in common purpose to secure the sanctuary of Irish waters for all whales and dolphins, the very nemesis of the hunts, which brought the great whales to the very verge of extinction in our time.

Unlike Ahab and his bedfellow revenge, or the monomaniacal hunt for profit, this unity of purpose giving rise to simultaneous and spontaneous whale sanctuary and guardians, was borne of a romantic love and truth such as that which sustained the troubadours of middle Europe in the Middle Ages, emerging from a very dark age. This group heralded an age of enlightenment for the welfare and well-being of whales and dolphins, built on its popular base, and representing so many inhabitants of the island of Ireland, has grown and developed the knowledge and science about these great animals.

Anyone who has attended whale rescues, strandings, or whale-watch events becomes transformed by the experience, passion, and dedication of this group and their all-consuming effort in the protection of whales.

In that room, at that moment in time, the stars were aligned, the opportunity was right, and the right people were there to seize it. To this day the state authorities have yet to register the sanctuary at an international level, but the hearts of those who brought the dream to reality live by its bounty and play in its waters, sustain it. *Gan tír, gan chroí!** Sanctuary has brought the benefits of tourism, employment, science, and enlightenment to many.

The *Taoiseach* of the day, one Hon. Charles gave it imprimatur and what legal standing it has, and his family donated *Celtic Mist*, the family yacht, to explore sanctuary the more. Sidney of England, father of modern whale-watching, exhorted other nations that the sanctuary "contagion spread." Under the guidance of Simon (not Peter but rock, nevertheless), a group of modern knights gathered around, including Padraig, Don, Dave, Emer, Marie, Sean, Mac, Johnny, Mick, and their successors, each with their own magic and bound by chivalric code as guardians of the sanctuary.

Sighting schemes, stranding schemes, rescues, whale-watching, ecotourism, science, and research, all flourished on the backs of the whales and this new sanctuary. Needless to say, the whales are safer and any new threats they face, the group faces with them. Sanctuary blesses giver and receiver alike.

Sanctuaries, like tectonic plates, are merging and coalescing, and in less than thirty years we have welcomed Antarctica; Antarctica extended; Indian Ocean; Ireland (as Europe's first); Ligurian Sea; Chile; with proposals for Mexico; Hawaiian islands; Great Barrier

Reef; South Atlantic; South Pacific and more! We have seen nation's accord constitutional and legal rights to nature!

As the spark was lit, the contagion has become a conflagration and the greatest unfinished tale of any group yet told in defence of the whale and promotion of sanctuary. The stories and successes of the Irish Whale and Dolphin Group* are now legion and ground-breaking at the global level.

It has been my great pleasure to journey with them a while, as along the road and in their company, one and all, I see the range of sanctuary extending.

The final page of World Whale Sanctuary is yet to be writ and there is no doubt that the Irish Whale and Dolphin Group con-tinue part of that glorious quest.

The moral of the tale must be: a group, however small, united and with sanctuary in their hearts, can chart the course of natural history and Earth for the good.

Epilogue: Songbird

In my attempts to write from simple animal experiences, I was to meet a creature of the spirit world as much as the animal world, and one entirely new to me.

It was a muse of legend. I had heard of such creatures, sprites, unicorns, other mythical creatures or manifestations of mind, but I did not know one. Does such a creature and guide appear for every creative effort in prose, poetry, music or art of any sort? If so, I must try to keep on composing, so wonderful and other-worldly is the experience. I am too new at this to know!

There are those in whose debt I remain for driving and inspiring the tales and the telling of them. Any magic captured came from the muse with the courage to overcome unforeseen obstacles.

The muse was a non-judgemental guide across the landscape of my memory and history of my life, and to make this journey, I was to be borne along by some of her stories as well as those of others.

The beauty of a story shared is that many more come by return.

In the hell and pain of darkened wards full of mutilated, suffering and dying young men, lying on shifts in their blood-stained clothes and bandaging, senses numbed by ether, exhaustion, and moaning, there often appeared a lantern followed by a soft presence and a quiet voice. It is said hope and peace became manifest in a smile from the "ladies of the lamp." For survivors of warfare, this was the real and first step on the road back to sanctuary, health, and happiness. By a smile, pain, loneliness, and grief were replaced by the courage to take strengthening steps to recovery and full potential. Legend has it, like the muse, the "lady of the lamp"* and her acolytes proved guide for innumerable casualties of war, returning to life from the darkest, most friendless, godless hours and experience of war's eternal night.

More than once in every life, there are such nights of the mind and a guide appears from an anonymous throng, offering no outward signs or spoken word to tell of their purpose … maybe just a smile.

There are cultures also who believe their spirit guide comes in a dream, in the form of an animal.

For the fox to be tamed or Exuperay to understand required their belief in the aforementioned Little Prince.

Muses come in many guises!

* * *

To be blessed by a muse, one must also believe.

The muse instructed me just "to be," who you are at any moment in time. Stories are in the moment and of the moment. Storytelling recalls the moment and gives it further life.

For a brief and wonderful while, I was to learn a little of my muse in shared stories. One wonder of this was to again find many things new.

I was to learn of a girl who liked to make tar babies from the steamy, hot, summery roads of her childhood; of song and dance routines with her brothers on a long kitchen draining board, behind drawn curtains on a Friday night after the parents went out, knocking back shots of bread soda with abandon, performing every song of the day in that transformed kitchen; of a beautiful young woman and survivor of good times and dark times; of the most heroic tales of motherhood her children would ever know; of a "wonderful friend to all the world," last seen playing with kittens and looking forward to further adventures.

Everyone meets such people, but to know them truly eyes must be open to their goodness.

I learned a muse is a multi-coloured nectar feeder, drinking fully of life and sharing all; it is an ephemeral creature like a butterfly, giving and giving till there is nothing left to give, who can, like a songbird, light up any company or cheer the world with a song, laugh, or smile. It is fragile and expects only in return that we grasp and live every moment joyously.

Lucky to have met one, I know now, like the Little Prince, my muse was real.

She guided my literary effort, but it could not fully do her justice. She showed me sanctuary in a simple smile and a place of peace for my little dalliance with literature, and if these stories resonate with any reader, I will be glad. They are my tribute, however awkward, to those I love, my encouragement to be aware of those we share life with. Without the muse, I could not have completed the attempt.

Muses are real! One guided me this way and remains my friend today.

I think she is a song and dance woman, and she has a name …

GLOSSARY

Back west: a local term for west, meaning beyond Dingle

Bear With Us: Canadian group dedicated to helping bears

Bedlam (or Bethlem): first hospital to specialise in mental illness; public could pay to view inmates

Bettystown: County Meath on Irish Sea, east coast of Ireland

Bogey: a hand-made or home-built cart to be pushed or pulled, usually from an old set of pram wheels

Bothies: homes

Born Free Foundation: dedicated to preserving wildlife in the wild; founded by Virginia McKenna and Bill Travers

Budlia: Dublin-ese for Buddleia/butterfly bush, which was introduced exotic to Ireland; Well, naturalised.

Clare: county on the west coast along Wild Atlantic Way

Clochán: little stone dwelling or bee-hive hut

Cannery Row: street lined with sardine canneries from John Steinbeck's Great Depression novel of same name

Delayed implantation: common to many species, where embryo development is suspended until more favourable conditions

Donnybrook: a fair in Dublin; gave its name to uproar and fighting

Dublin: capital city of Ireland

Exuperay: French novelist, early aviator, and author of classic, *The Little Prince*

Fadó, Fadó: long, long ago

Fingal: regarded as the "thirty-third" county of Ireland, on east coast north of Dublin; Ireland has thirty-two counties

Flipper's trainer: Ric O'Barry dedicates his life to ending dolphin captivity

Gael: a native Irish

Gall: a foreigner

Gan tír, gan chroí: meaning without a country, without a heart

Gardaí: Irish police

Holt: an otter den or home

"Humanity Dick" Martin: Irish member of British House of Lords, introduced 1st anti-cruelty legislation, the 1822 Martin Act

In our gift: in our ability to provide or "gift"

Irish Seal Sanctuary: national wildlife welfare organisation and urban legend empowering people to care for wildlife in their own communities

Irish Whale and Dolphin Group: organization dedicated to the protection and study of cetaceans in Irish waters

Ishmael and **Ahab**: narrator and nemesis to the great white whale in Melville's classic, *Moby Dick*

Joe Smart: a wonderful zookeeper and early mentor

Lady of the lamp: Florence Nightingale, and her nurses, ministered through Crimean War and were dedicated to improving public health and hospital care.

Marla: plasticine; modern equivalent is play dough

Off the mother: off milk and done nursing

On the button: accurate or on the mark

Orwell: British author, prophet of dystopian future as characterised by concern for social injustice, which was famously expressed in *Animal Farm* and *1984*

Penny dropped: to become suddenly aware

Rationing years: Ireland was neutral in WWII, and there was much rationing.

Ros Muc: a village located on west coast of Ireland

Round and Martello towers: watch-out and defence towers from early monastic and Napoleonic periods respectively

Rural Ireland: national movement to conserve rural traditions and ways of life

Sett: a badger burrow or home

Silent Spring: Rachel Carson's prophetic book on environment

Sin scéal eile, le leabhar eile: another story for another book

Skerries: a coastal village in North County Dublin, once a thriving fishing port

St. Patrick's Day: an Irish national feast day and holiday celebrated on March 17th.

Sunshiners: volunteers and children holidaying in Sunshine House(s) run by the Vincent de Paul Charity to give city children who might not otherwise experience a holiday time out of the city and by the sea

Taoiseach: leader; Irish equivalent of a prime minister

Titbits: morsels or tasty scraps

Tom Beag: meaning "small Tom"

Torai Island: an inhabited island off Donegal in Northwest Ireland

Wains: very young children

FURTHER READING

Brendan"s website: www.brendanprice.com Please pass on these stories when read and share yours in return.

Chief Seattle's 1854 Oration

Silent Spring, Rachel Carson

The Little Prince, Antoine de Saint-Exupery

Humanity Dick Martin, "King of Connemara", Shevawn Lynam

Dublin Zoo: An Illustrated History, Catherine de Courcy

The People of the Sea, David Thomson

LAUDATO SI: on care for our common home, Pope Francis

LANUGO: (Film) 100 Years of Grey Seal Protection https://www.youtube.com/channel/UCBMnb0XW0jkihPYf2M-MlvOQ

Moby Dick, Herman Melville

The Wild Atlantic Way: www.wildatlanticway.com Tourism Trail, Atlantic coast, Ireland

Irish Society for Protection of Animals: www.ispca.ie

Irish Seal Sanctuary (Facebook): https://www.facebook.com/Irish-Seal-Sanctuary-196564313813250/

Irish Seal Sanctuary (website): www.irishsealsanctuary.ie

Bear With Us: www.bearwithus.org

Born Free: www.bornfree.org.uk

Fondation Franz Weber: www.ffw.ch

Ric O'Barry Dolphin Project: https://dolphinproject.net/
The Cove (film) http://www.thecovemovie.com/richardobarry.htm
Irish Heritage Council: http://www.heritagecouncil.ie/home/
Irish Wildlife Trust: http://www.iwt.ie/
Bioweb: http://bioweb.ie/
Irish Whale and Dolphin Group: http://www.iwdg.ie/
Wildlife Waystation: http://wildlifewaystation.org/

Author Biography

Brendan Price grew up in the new and emerging suburbs on the south side of Dublin, now living rurally on the north side.

He received a Newman education at Catholic University School and University College Dublin, graduating in Agricultural Science in reverse of the flight from the land. He is a suburbanite retracing an ancient journey.

In the Dublin of Brendan's childhood, city and suburbs, farmland and wilderness, land and sea, were all connected and collectively represented a hedge-school of conservation, from which he and his peers graduated backwards. His intimacy with our natural world and passion in its defence was nurtured there.

Worldwide exploding populations and inequitable voracious demand for resources have left the frontiers of wilderness and strongholds of wildlife in accelerated retreat. At these frontiers there is always conflict, and Brendan is never far from it.

Brendan came to public attention as enfant terrible and cause of the Dublin Zoo Enquiry. He secured the ratification in Ireland of the UN Convention for International Trade in Endangered Species (CITES). He is founder of the Irish Seal Sanctuary and co-founder of the Irish Whale and Dolphin Group. He is controversial and popular, challenging animal abuse and defending wildlife. Like Groucho Marx, he is proud to have been "thrown out of all the best places."

Often challenging conventional science, conservation, and welfare, Brendan is an advocate of wildlife welfare, the intangible influences of wildlife on us as a species, and the healing potential of our earthly home. A naturalist's curiosity over a lifetime brought some answers, some insights, but also many questions. Brendan continues to explore this changing world, challenging our stewardship and pricking our consciences. He invites you to explore with him through folk-memory and story, the struggle to resolve wildlife conflicts, believing those who speak for the most vulnerable—the remaining wildlife—speak for humanity.

Review Requested:
If you loved this book, would you please provide a review at
Amazon.com?

CPSIA information can be obtained at www.ICGtesting.com
Printed in the USA
LVOW08s1421100716

495760LV00002BA/318/P